Together in Hope
50 Years of Lutheran World Relief

John W. Bachman

Lutheran World Relief
New York, New York

Distributed by Kirk House Publishers
Minneapolis, Minnesota

TOGETHER IN HOPE
50 Years of Lutheran World Relief

Cover design: Judy Swanson

Library of Congress Cataloging-in-Publication data

Bachman, John W., 1916-
    Together in Hope: 50 Years of Lutheran World Relief / John W. Bachman
        p. cm.
    Includes bibliographical references and index.
    ISBN 1-886513-01-5 (alk. paper)
    1. Lutheran World Relief—History.   2. Church work the poor—Lutheran   Church.   3.International relief—History—20th century.
    I. Title.
BX8074.B4B33 1995
361.7'5'088241—dc20   95-3114
                                                          CIP

Distributed by Kirk House Publishers, P.O. Box 39759, Minneapolis, MN 55439

Manufactured in the U.S.A.

Contents

To combat compassion fatigue, courage found in the history of LWR.

To serve suffering European Lutherans after World War II, LWR is created and staffed; money is raised, clothing and bedding collected.

After changes in U.S. policy opposed to aiding former enemy, enormous effort undertaken to serve the neediest without qualification.

Original vision stretched by new conflicts and catastrophes. LCMS joins; carloads of commodities, quilts and clothing are shipped.

Expansion of services to "extended family," far beyond Lutheranism.

New policies formulated; concern for continuing financial support.

Development becomes at least as important as relief. A "Hope Corps" ventures into areas such as Vietnam, Korea, Taiwan, India.

All projects to deal with locally recognized needs, carried on by the people themselves in a genuine partnership; development diversified.

Foreword

During my whole ordained ministry, Lutheran World Relief has been a part of my identity as a Christian of Lutheran persuasion. The same has been true since the end of World War II for hosts of Lutherans in the United States. Not all of us paid attention to the organization through which the work was done; but many of us were proud that our church affiliation meant we were reaching out to persons in lands less affluent than ours, and we were doing it as an expression of our Christian faith.

Now in 1995, it is fifty years since Lutheran World Relief began its work. A third generation has begun to assume leadership in the churches that support Lutheran World Relief. Before the memory of earlier generations is no longer current, it is time to put the history into print.

John W. Bachman was chosen to write this history because of his vast experience in the field of communication and his first-hand knowledge of Lutheran World Relief. The author of five previously published books, he has been engaged in the teaching and practice of communication on the faculty of Union Theological Seminary in New York, in the national offices of the American Lutheran Church, and in policy-making for the Lutheran World Federation. He has had the opportunity to visit LWR projects in many parts of the world and served on the agency's board for five years. I am deeply grateful to Bachman for the countless hours he has spent digging into files in archives, reading reports, minutes, and correspondence, and interviewing people. The drafting and redrafting, which have resulted in this volume of history, represent a labor of love from a man who has shared deeply in the Christian identity which has included LWR.

An anniversary is a time for celebrating life. What a life Lutheran World Relief has had during its fifty years! It was a life that lived first in church leaders whom I have considered heroes of the faith. They believed that the evil which perpetrated war should not have the last word; nor should the destruction that shattered the evil. They were leaders who worked to re-establish relationships among Lutherans of all nations and, in this way, to heal a broken world. They served to make survival possible for people who had lost almost everything. They shaped invigorating motivation for many of us and pointed us to new, constructive goals. I am forever indebted to those stalwart ambassadors for Christ and I am grateful that their memory will be preserved in this history of Lutheran World Relief.

In those early postwar years, although I worked at a great distance from the pioneering work and leadership of Lutheran World Relief, LWR was for me a means of expressing the universal message of the church, a fulfillment of the worldwide fellowship of believers who were concerned not only for themselves but for all people. Important as private prayer was in my life, LWR presented a challenge to move out from my prayer bench, beyond personal concerns and associations, to contribute to people whom I would never know personally. Overworked as I was, as pastor of a growing local parish, LWR called on me to share in prayers and offerings for people outside my locality, indeed, beyond the synodical and national boundaries of my church organization. Lutheran World Relief was an effective force in helping me to realize an identity as a citizen of the world and as a member of the church's universal priesthood.

In recent years, more intimate identification with Lutheran World Relief has kept me abreast of important new chapters in the history of Christian diaconal service. Now the reader of this volume can review that history.

After participating in the mammoth reconstruction in war-torn lands, LWR moved on with history. Since the United States was the greatest power in the free world, our nation assumed responsibility for maintaining order and economic viability globally. We Lutherans in America tried to keep pace and do our share. We had an agency in LWR that could be counted on to respond in each crisis that occurred. When headlines in the newspapers and reports on radio and television portrayed the horror of a disaster, our Christian consciences could respond with contributions to Lutheran World Relief. We could be sure we would be present through an agency that bore the identifying name of our church.

Lutheran World Relief, like other agencies engaged in overseas relief work, learned from experience, expanded its role, and dealt with complex new issues, as this history reveals. I am grateful for what I learned from Lutheran World Relief and the way the history now records these lessons for further and wider consideration.

For me, Lutheran World Relief has lived on Jesus' story of the Good Samaritan. No human barriers would keep it from sharing material ministrations with those in need—not nationality nor ethnic distinctions, not differences of religion, not distance, not lack of acquaintance with the needy person; all features in Jesus' story.

The people whom Lutheran World Relief calls to my attention are not always people that I immediately recognize as my kind of people. Sometimes they are citizens of a nation that has been an enemy of my country. Or they belong to a culture which is considered inferior and degraded by those of us who prize our Euro-American civilization. They might be ardent adherents of a religion other than Christianity. In most cases they are people who could easily be branded unattractive in their state of malnutrition or disease or impoverishment or whatever dehumanizing condition. Lutheran World Relief calls me to a compassion that leaps over my prejudices and instinctive revulsions. I have to admit that the call is consistent with Christian faith. In fact, Lutheran World Relief exists because Lutheran Christians have received the call from Jesus Christ. LWR is a product of faith active in love. As expressed in that refrain in the popular hymn, it provides the means whereby, "They will know we are Christians by our love."

An anniversary is more than a time to reflect on the past. To be sure, the history of Lutheran World Relief must very appreciatively laud the great leaders, decisions, and deeds in its fifty years of service. The history can stir us to gratitude for all that God has made possible through our predecessors and through us. We will be reminded of how much can be accomplished when Christians work together. Yet, reflecting on the past dare not become an exercise in self-satisfaction, much less self-righteousness. The history reminds us of the kind of world we live in and how impossible it is for us to expect enduring security and comfort in any withdrawn, neat, and protective isolation. As we look at the past through the eyes of faith, we are reminded of God's presence, purpose, and power. The future opens before us with challenging possibilities for us as Lutheran people in congregations and church bodies to testify to our faith in the darkest corners of the world through the work of Lutheran World Relief.

Robert J. Marshall

Acknowledgments

To trace the fifty years of Lutheran World Relief's history, printed material was readily available from three major sources: the archives of the Evangelical Lutheran Church in America, the library of Luther Seminary in St. Paul, Minnesota, and the files in the New York offices of LWR.

In Chicago ELCA archivist Elisabeth Wittman, Steven Bean, her assistant until recently, and Russell Deloney left nothing undone to locate documents for me. Much of the early material and five photographs for this book came from the Helen M. Knubel Archives of Cooperative Lutheranism, now a part of the archives of the ELCA. The Oral History Collection, to which Alice Kendrick had contributed so much, contained illuminating references from different observers.

Librarian Norman Wente at Luther Seminary and Bruce Eldevik, reference librarian, cooperated in every possible way.

In New York and elsewhere the documentation was supplemented and illuminated by conversations. Staff members, both present and past, were not only responsive in interviews but were so helpful in tracing detailed information that they encouraged me in what might otherwise have become a rather laborious task; they were, unanimously, not only knowledgeable, but determined, committed to LWR's mission, and enthusiastic about their participation in it. I will simply recognize contributors from the current staff in alphabetical order: June Braun, Milton Briggs, Carol Capps, Frank Conlon, Candy Eng, Peggy Erxmeyer, Ophelia Farmer, John Fasio, Jonathan Frerichs, Ann Fries, Roland Fritchman, Gloria Garcia, Kenneth Killen, Carol Seischab, Terri Speirs, Joseph Sprunger, Anna Belle and Gene Thiemann, Jeff Whisenant, and Kathryn Wolford.

Among former staff members Ove Nielsen and Robert Busche were especially helpful because of their long and intimate association with LWR. Other valuable contributions came from Jerry Aaker, Abner and Martha Batalden, James Claypool, Robert Cottingham, William Dingler, Stewart Herman, Walter Jensen, Carl Mau, Rollin Shaffer, and Edna Wagschal. Norman Barth shared especially significant insights.

Edwin Nerger recalled board meetings as far back as the fifties; Robert Marshall and Morris Sorenson refreshed my own recollections from the middle years, and among the present directors I was able to make connections with Richard Krenzke, Charles Lutz, Betty Lee Nyhus, Norman Sell, and Mark Thomsen.

Others consulted include Hallie Confer, Oswald Hoffman, Howard Hong, Robert E. A. Lee, and Philip Johnson.

From among all of these contributors the following have reviewed the manuscript and made helpful suggestions: Robert Marshall, Norman Barth, Kathryn Wolford, Norman Sell, Charles Lutz, and Jonathan Frerichs.

Leonard Flachman and Karen Walhof of Kirk House Publishers and their associates have been generous with their time and facilities in the production of this book. Cheryl D. Crocket provided valuable assistance in the final editing.

Elsie Bachman was supportive throughout the project, assisted with research, and was a reliable proofreader. She has graciously survived the experience of living with someone who was spending so much of his time in the past.

John W. Bachman

Introduction: Hope Confronts Despair

Ethiopia...Sudan...Somalia...Rwanda...Bosnia...Haiti.... The litany of woe is unending. Poverty and hunger are compounded by conflict and accompanied by disease. Winners and losers inhabit the same wastelands.

At the turn of the century India will have a population of a billion, with 400 million estimated to fall below the country's poverty line. Needs in Cambodia and Vietnam are still enormous. In Iraq the aftermath of war and persecution of minorities creates instability.

In Latin America large sections of the population have no place in the emerging marketplace of the hemisphere, prolonging the persistence of widespread poverty and suffering.

Altogether, then, more than a billion of the world's people live in poverty, with other estimates more than doubling this figure. One hundred million are homeless. One hundred fifty million children under five years (one in three) are malnourished and almost 13 million children die each year before their fifth birthdays.[1]

Overcoming Compassion Fatigue

Such a barrage of facts can be overwhelming. Pictures of starving children make a numbing impact on us. The needs are so great and our personal resources so limited by comparison, that one understandable response is despair. What can one person, or one faith community do that will make any difference? Do we not have enough problems at home without taking on the burdens of the world?

For Christians such a response to global needs cannot be considered. Poverty, homelessness, and hunger call upon us to minister to the needy as to Christ himself. Injustice and oppression are offenses against God. The resources of creation are blessings to be preserved and shared, not exploited by a few. Others may despair, but we confront that temptation with hope, knowing that, "with God, all things are possible."

The primary instrument through which Lutherans in America confront the apparently impossible demands of global needs is Lutheran World Relief. Beginning in 1945 simply as an agency offering relief to devastated Europe after World War II, Lutheran World Relief has discovered and accepted a much broader mission. Adapting to changing circumstances, LWR has moved beyond relief into development of material resources, then into development of people and communities. All of this has been undertaken in close partnership with global organizations, especially the Lutheran World Federation, but also with local community agencies. The affluent have been enlisted to work together in hope with the poorest of the poor.

The following chapters will feature stories of a pilgrimage through 50 years of diligent action. Readers will be prodded into wrestling with issues that have prompted thoughtful deliberation at various stages in the growth of Lutheran World Relief. In the end, LWR should emerge as a lively enterprise poised to deal competently with the incredibly complex tasks facing such agencies today.

How Did They Do It?

To appreciate the emergence of this human institution, it is important to begin by recalling the predicament of the founders. Problems confronting Lutherans in America at the end of World War II appeared to be just as formidable as any existing today.

In 1945 European cities and countrysides from London to Moscow and Leningrad were devastated. Germany was described as a "human vacuum of unspeakable suffering made worse by millions of displaced people on the move to nowhere." [2] Starvation and disease stalked conquered, liberated, and victorious nations. Beyond Europe there was extensive destruction in northern Africa, Ethiopia, China, parts of Japan, and some Pacific islands.

The reaction of sheltered Americans to this crisis could have been one of despair, but our spiritual fathers and mothers took a far different course. Their faith motivated them to respond with vision and determination. Their amazing accomplishments through Lutheran World Relief serve as an inspiration for us today. What they and their successors learned through 50 years of Lutheran World Relief experiences provides guidance for us in preparing to deal with global concerns in the 21st century. Admittedly, the founders' response was motivated partly, at least in the beginning, by a feeling of kinship.

A Family Crisis

At the close of World War II vast numbers of the suffering people in Europe were in Germany or other European countries with at least a heritage of Lutheranism. Most Lutherans in the United States traced their ancestry to those same regions, and many still had relatives abroad for whom they were understandably concerned. So it was not difficult to appeal for compassion toward brothers and sisters in trouble. In fact, toward the war's end individuals and congregations were pleading with leaders of American Lutheranism to find ways to send aid abroad.

Fortunately, there were existing channels to begin this process. For many years representatives of the world's Lutheran churches had been meeting periodically to explore common beliefs and concerns. Already after World War I there had been a joint effort to provide assistance to suffering survivors, leading to the organization in the United States of the National Lutheran Council in 1918 and to the formation of the Lutheran World Convention in 1923. Nearly all Lutheran churches in America except The Lutheran Church—Missouri Synod and the Evangelical Joint Synod of Wisconsin and Other States participated in both, and the National Lutheran Council, in practice, served as the American section of the Lutheran World Convention. When World War II made the global body virtually inoperative, the Council took many actions on behalf of the global Convention until, in 1947, the Lutheran World Federation came into existence, replacing the Convention.

Between the two wars the NLC lost momentum and barely survived the depression. When, in 1930, Ralph H. Long became executive director, his first task was to make a drastic cut in the Council's budget, but he was prepared for both saving and raising money because he had been an able stewardship secretary of the Joint Synod of Ohio. Osborne Hauge, a chronicler of that period, commented, "His willingness to take over responsibility for the work of an agency that many expected to expire within a year is a tribute to the quality of his faith and his determination." [1] Long did have a vision of what Lutherans could do together, and under his leadership the National Lutheran Council became strong enough to create and nurture an agency as ambitious as Lutheran World Relief.

Surveying the Needs

Long participated actively in the deliberations of the Lutheran World Convention and when war disrupted those relationships he was determined to restore them as soon as possible. Already during the war he instituted annual efforts to raise money for ministry to U.S. military service personnel and for support of missions cut off from their European sponsors. Designated as Lutheran World Action in 1940, the appeals raised nearly 25 million dollars by 1949.[2] Long directed the first appeals himself but Paul Empie, his assistant, took charge beginning in 1945.

With the end of the war approaching, Long and others realized that it was time to stretch this sense of compassion into more extensive service abroad. Long was always hopeful of enlisting The Lutheran Church—Missouri Synod in cooperative efforts and, when he and President P. O. Bersell of the Augustana Synod planned, in early 1945 before the end of the war, to survey conditions in Europe, they were joined by Lawrence Meyer of The Lutheran Church—Missouri Synod. For six weeks in March and April they visited England, Scotland, Sweden, France, and Switzerland, a trip made possible through facilities of the U.S. Air Transport Command. They met with representatives of all the larger Lutheran church groups in Europe, hearing incredible stories of suffering in the occupied countries and in all war-devastated lands.

In Geneva they had access to a wide range of valuable information from the skeleton staff of the World Council of Churches, which had been in the process of formation since 1937 but would not be constituted until 1948. In view of the enormity of the task ahead, it was obvious that there had to be the broadest possible cooperation among all Christians. Churches that could act alone in many endeavors simply could not be effective by themselves in relief and rehabilitation. Swedish leaders were ready immediately to participate in joint efforts and a Reconstruction Committee from the World Council of Churches was beginning its work.

When the delegation returned, Bersell wrote, "We have come back with a great sorrow. The total devastation, physical and spiritual, is indescribable and unappraisable.... The relief of the physical need and the rebuilding of Europe will tax the capacity of the united efforts of the whole Christian world (what there is left of it)."[3]

Seeing the importance of regular contacts between the U. S. and Europe, Long recruited a long-time friend, Sylvester C. Michelfelder, to go to Geneva on leave from his congregation in Toledo, Ohio. At first he represented only the American Section of the Lutheran World Convention, but later he became the acting executive secretary for the Convention's successor agency, the Lutheran World Federation. In addition, he soon accepted an assignment by the World Council of Churches to organize a Division of Material Aid as part of its Department of Reconstruction and Interchurch Aid. He resigned from his pastorate and in all of his international offices was a valuable resource for what became Lutheran World Relief.

A New Corporation

Ralph Long realized also that, for such an international venture, a new agency was needed. The National Lutheran Council's Division of Welfare, established in 1939, was a source of valuable skills and information, but the complexities of global relationships and international shipping posed distinctive problems. Above all, it was clear that governments, both U.S. and others, would be deeply involved in providing access and possible funding, and an organization with independent legal standing would be in the best position to enter into the necessary agreements.

Needing reliable legal advice, Long turned to a person with whom, by a strange coincidence, he had become acquainted and in whom he had complete confidence. Michael Markel had been a young lawyer employed by the Frigidaire Company in New York to deal with complaints. When a family in Brooklyn refused to make payments because their new refrigerator was not working properly, Markel went to confront the purchasers and met the owner, Ralph Long. When the two discovered that they were Lutherans and alumni of Capital University, it was the beginning of a deep friendship. It also led to enlistment of Markel in a mission of service on behalf of Lutheranism over more than a quarter of a century.

In 1945 the U.S. Congress passed legislation establishing a War Relief Control Board to register and regulate voluntary relief agencies permitted to deal and ship abroad after the war. Long went to Washington to learn the requirements to qualify for such designation and on his return arranged for Markel and Franklin Clark Fry, then newly elected president of the United Lutheran Church in America, to have lunch with him. Markel was asked how an agency could be incorporated most expeditiously for the immediate purpose and he indicated that this could be accomplished under the Membership Corporation Law, and that the three of them could do this. It was agreed that the number of directors should be increased to five, and the names of Long's assistant, Paul Empie, and S. Frederick Telleen were added to those of the three present. Fry would become president, Long secretary, and Telleen treasurer, a role in which he served with a number of other religious organizations. This self-perpetuating board made it possible for individual Christian citizens to act on their faith in ventures with the government without any threat to the precarious church-state relationship.

Markel raised the question of funding for the agency but Fry answered, "You get us incorporated and I'll see about the money." [4] It was actually the income from Lutheran World Action appeals that provided most of the money for a long time, but Fry also remained vigorous and influential in his promotion of financial support.

The necessary documents were filed in New York on October 11, 1945, and incorporation became official on October 24. The Certificate of Incorporation made it clear that the new agency was being formed to receive and distribute "gifts of clothing, food, medical supplies and other commodities...for relief, rehabilitation, reconstruction and welfare arising from war-created needs...." Lutheran World Relief thus became a legally separate entity but retained its personal and financial ties with the National Lutheran Council, and was adopted immediately in January by the American Section of the Lutheran World Convention as its channel for material aid. Recognizing both of these ties, the LWR Board of Directors was expanded to include the presidents of five member bodies of the Council and four other pastors.[5] In practice, all eight presidents of the NLC member churches exercised a voice in early LWR affairs because much of the financial support was channeled through the Council. By that time the membership included the American Lutheran Church, Augustana Synod, Danish Lutheran Church, Evangelical Lutheran Church, Finnish Suomi Synod, Lutheran Free Church, United Evangelical Lutheran Church, and United Lutheran Church in America.

Markel was correct; this legal action paved the way for government recognition. After joining the American Council of Voluntary Agencies for Foreign Service, LWR became a founding member of both the Council of Relief Agencies Licensed for Operation in Germany (CRALOG) and Licensed Agencies for Relief in Asia (LARA).

Lutherans in Canada recognized the same needs and established Canadian Lutheran World Relief on March 14, 1946. The two agencies have participated in many common ventures through the years. From the beginning LWR has also cooperated actively with Church World Service, the relief agency founded by many Protestant and Orthodox churches, later incorporated in the National Council of Churches in the U.S.A.

Organizing for Action

Lutheran World Relief's original five directors were prepared to meet regularly to set directions for the new agency, but all were otherwise occupied with full-time responsibilities. They quickly enlisted another executive, also fully employed, to take charge of the daily operation. Clarence E. Krumbholz, the executive secretary of the NLC's Division of Welfare, was undoubtedly more knowledgeable about relief than any of the incorporators, and he shared with them the deep conviction that something should be done immediately. He therefore agreed to supervise the establishment of an office with essential staff to begin carrying on the intended work. Since at least two of the officers, Long and Fry, were expected to be absent often, he was also named chairman of an administrative committee to include Paul Empie, Telleen, and anticipated staff members.

Krumbholz was soon devoting more than half his time to organizing the work. While acquiring the necessary information to deal with a complicated situation, he was answering a volume of correspondence, issuing letters of appeal and information to pastors, and making arrangements for use of warehouses.[6] Through his many contacts around the country, he was able to call on a chain of Lutheran social agencies to help interpret the work of LWR.

Krumbholz was very influential at a critical point in Lutheran World Relief's beginning and made a major contribution toward the direction taken by the agency. He led in the adoption of at least one policy that has never been changed: LWR would not become involved in the shipment of packages to individual recipients. There was pressure for this, of course, from American relatives of Lutherans abroad, and European black marketeers were soliciting funds for such packages, which could then be sold at exorbitant prices. Krumbholz calculated that if the $10 spent to send one package would be contributed toward the cost of a major shipment, more than twice as many needs would be served. He identified this as an expression of thoughtful stewardship.

The administrative committee retained its name but within two years consisted of the original directors. When Ralph Long died suddenly in February, 1948, Krumbholz was elected to replace him on the board and as secretary. Paul Empie took Long's place as executive secretary of the National Lutheran Council, and continued the remarkable leadership of his predecessor.

Daily administration of the LWR office was gradually changing. In 1946 Krumbholz had employed a young U.S. Army veteran, Bernard Confer, to assist him. Confer was a graduate of Penn State University and had worked for two years in the Pennsylvania Department of Public Assistance before going into the military. He was so efficient in his work with LWR that, already in 1947, he was given the title of administrative assistant. In 1953 he became executive director, a position in which he served for 28 more years.

Shortly after being added to the staff, Confer made a subtraction from it. The first secretary hired for LWR was a young woman who had just completed three years in the Coast Guard and became interested in the agency by hearing Sylvester Michelfelder, at a Reformation rally in New York, paint a somber picture of the war-torn countries of Europe. Hallie Baker and Confer were assigned nearby desks and in less than two years they were married.[7] Soon after that, Hallie Baker Confer resigned her position but has maintained a deep interest in Lutheran World Relief throughout the ensuing decades.

War's End

The visit to Europe by Long, Bersell, and Meyer had provided a glimpse of the enormous task ahead. After their return, V-E Day on May 7 and V-J Day on August 14 officially ended the conflict in 1945 and opened the way for a more thorough study of what should be done. Another delegation was appointed, with Long being accompanied by Fry and President J. A. Aasgaard of the Norwegian Lutheran Church of America, then in the process of becoming the Evangelical Lutheran Church. Lawrence Meyer again represented The Lutheran Church—Missouri Synod, along with President John Behnken. They were to confer with church leaders in France, Belgium, and Switzerland, then go to Germany for ten days of consultation with top German Lutheran church officials. They hoped to work toward a closely integrated program of relief and reconstruction through unified world Lutheran action. The three NLC-LWR representatives were then to go to Copenhagen for a meeting December 13 and 14 of the Lutheran World Convention Executive Committee, the first since before the war.[8]

An awkward situation arose within the delegation. As it happened, the Missouri Synod representatives received their travel documents before the others and sailed to Germany to make their own plans. Franklin Clark Fry, always a stickler for protocol and never one to enjoy being second in anything, suspected intrigue and, when the groups encountered each other in Frankfurt, proceeded to excoriate Behnken. Behnken was mystified and Fry was later persuaded that Behnken had not been responsible for the mixup. When the two next met, Fry was so kind, generous, and deferential that Behnken said, "Dr. Fry treated me as if I were his father." [9] Even though LCMS did not affiliate actively with LWR until the fifties, there were many instances of cooperation from the beginning.

The returning delegation brought reaffirmation of all that was feared. The devastation to both people and environment was beyond description. The needs were overwhelming but the opportunity for Christians to follow in their Lord's path of service was equally clear and striking.

Immediate Need

Even before this delegation reported, Lutherans in America were beginning to respond to the desolation abroad. Congregations were notified, "Every old suit, overcoat, every suit of underwear, every available blanket should be gathered together for shipment at the earliest opportunity."

It was not immediately feasible to send food from America but this would soon be possible and money was needed to purchase, store, and ship all useful supplies. Michelfelder managed to arrange for a shipment from Sweden to Germany of $100,000 worth of flour, coffee, roast beef, and rolled oats. Medicine was available from Switzerland and shoes were also procured and sent.[10]

Paul Empie sent "An Open Letter to Lutherans in America" explaining that the international organization, United Nations Relief and Rehabilitation Agency, could not possibly meet the needs and that it was even prevented by law from helping people in Germany and Austria. He opened the letter by asking, "Can we interest each of you in saving a human life? It has come to that." As if writing in 1995, he wrote, "The story has been told and pictured so often that one's senses tend to become calloused. We are apt to ease our consciences by saying, 'What can we hope to do? We can't achieve for 20,000,000 people what the United Nations are unable to do!' Yet should we not try because we may be able to rescue only, say, 200,000 who are our brethren?" At this time there was still considerable emphasis on the Lutheran family abroad and American congregations were assured that, during the final two months of 1945, all contributions for Lutheran World Action would go to relief in Europe.[11]

Response from Lutherans in America was immediate and personal. One lady from Oregon, sending a check for $1,000, wrote, "Realizing the great need and suffering of the people in Europe, I enclose this check sent with a thankful heart for the many blessings God has given me. I pray his blessing will go with this offering to help save some lives." From Bryant, Iowa, a farmer gave the $267.00 check he had received from the government's Commodity Credit Corporation in payment for his beef production.[12]

The response was also challenging to the tiny Lutheran World Relief staff. Cash and checks poured in to the offices, and tons of clothing and bedding arrived at a warehouse in Easton, Pennsylvania, where arrangements had been made to handle LWR shipping. The gifts made possible rapid action. Within the first three months of 1946, 2,260 bales of clothing and bedding, plus 245 bags of shoes, were shipped to five countries. Two thirds of these went to Finland, with Holland, Czechoslovakia, Belgium (for Latvian refugees), and Yugoslavia receiving the rest. By mid-March there were an estimated 20,000 bales of clothing, or 2 million pounds, available in the warehouse.[13]

Luther Kirsch, a young man who would soon go to Finland for reconstruction work with the Quakers, was handling shipping details, and staff members of the NLC's Welfare Division contributed many hours of assistance.

Sensing both the extent of the need abroad and the depth of concern among Lutherans in America, leaders set—and met—a combined goal of 10 million dollars for the 1946 and 1947 Lutheran World Action financial appeals. After 1947 the goals were reduced but still averaged several million dollars annually. Most of the income went from the National Lutheran Council directly to the Lutheran World Federation for recovery of both churches and individuals. LWR's grants from the NLC, supplemented by other income, especially gifts in kind, were enough support for significant service. The Emergency Planning Council of The Lutheran Church—Missouri Synod was carrying on its own overseas relief efforts but contributed

$66,000 to LWR in 1946 and later, as we shall see, shared proportionately in LWR finances. The Plattdeutsche Volksfest Vereins of Brooklyn and New York were regular contributors.

Beginning in 1949, an attempt was made to coordinate LWA giving with "One Great Hour of Sharing," a national ingathering promoted by Protestant, Roman Catholic, and Orthodox Churches. National media were employed to encourage participation on the fourth Sunday in Lent. Some Lutheran congregations responded, but others preferred to stay with a Sunday in May, designated by LWA, usually Mother's Day.

Contributors were inspired by knowing that, even in Europe, Lutherans were stretching resources to share with the needy. Swedish Christians, for example, were spending $500,000 a month trying to sustain brothers and sisters in neighboring lands. In Norway neighboring Swedes were feeding 137,000 children, 83,000 seniors, and 23,000 youth.[14]

Along with contributions, letters raising questions also arrived in New York, and both Long, before his death, and then Krumbholz tried to answer them. To the natural question as to why, in the face of so much hunger and even starvation, food was not yet being included in the shipments, they could explain that some food and medicines were being supplied by LWR through purchases made in Europe. To one overriding question, however, there was not yet a satisfactory answer at the end of 1945: when will we be able to send relief directly to Germany?

The German Question

The United Nations Relief and Rehabilitation Administration, the massive international organization created by the United Nations as a humanitarian effort following victory, was never intended to give aid to former enemies. With the partition of Germany, the occupying military forces of Britain, France, and the United States were given responsibility for whatever relief was provided to residents of their respective zones in western Germany.

For the American zone, official policy was very restrictive, based on the belief that American citizens were opposed to any generosity toward the residents of a nation whose army had brought such destruction on Europe. There seemed to be no collective memory of the fact that it was just such a shortsighted, vindictive policy following World War I that paved the way for Hitler to gain enough power to repeat the earlier disaster.

Sylvester Michelfelder reported from Geneva toward the end of 1945 that he saw a tragedy unfolding that would exceed the tragedy of the war itself. He had gone to Switzerland in the belief that his primary task would be to aid in bringing the churches back to life, but he soon concluded that it must be "bread first—catechisms later." He wrote, "Three or four times as many people will die of starvation and cold and beatings this winter as died in the war itself unless there is an immediate change in the attitude of the United Nations who are now the victors. I see hundreds of thousands of deported people from the Baltic provinces in makeshift German camps, with no promise of ever having homes again. If they are forced to go back by the Russians, they will be treated as political enemies and sent to Siberia or shot.... To seek new homes overseas is almost impossible."

Michelfelder saw an example of attempted "ethnic cleansing" in "the fleeing millions whose only crime is that they speak German.... Driven from place to place like dangerous animals, each move finds them worse off than before." [1] From his post in Geneva Michelfelder was able to send only small amounts of food and medicine to Germany and Austria by way of the Red Cross.

American Lutherans, especially those whose ancestors had come from Germany, were dismayed by their government's policy. They joined with members of many other denominations in protests to Washington and, already in November, the President's War Relief Control Board appeared to open the way for shipment of aid, but the permission extended only to United Nations nationals or Nazi victims, excluding most of the population. There was still confusion over the whole matter.[2] Ironically, before the situation was clarified in Washington, the British government announced that there was "no objection to importation of gifts of all sorts" for relief of suffering in the British Zone of Occupation.[3]

Under auspices of the Federal Council of Churches of Christ in America, another delegation of church leaders was appointed to study the situation in Germany. Franklin Fry was one of the three appointed, along with Methodist Bishop G. Bromley Oxnam and Protestant Episcopal Bishop Henry Knox Sherrill. They were guided in extensive travels by Stewart Herman, a Lutheran on the staff of the World Council of Churches. Herman also represented LWR on still another survey team whose visit was authorized by President Truman and endorsed by the U.S. State and War Departments. In his book, *The Rebirth of the German Church*, published already in 1946, Herman provided a graphic, detailed description of the horrible conditions existing in Germany and eastern Europe at that time.[4]

The report from the church executives underlined the unspeakable hardships they had observed, and pleaded for a more understanding approach to the people of Germany. A congressional committee, returning from Europe at the same time, bluntly concluded, "If a 'hard peace' requires the elimination of eight or ten millions of Germans, it would be much more humane to eliminate them at once." [5]

Visit to the White House

The controversy apparently came to a head when Oxnam, Fry, and Roswell Barnes of the Federal Council of Churches met with President Truman in the White House on January 16, 1946. Fry himself, in a letter to Stewart Herman, summarized the conversation after it had become his turn to speak: "I rehearsed the encouragement which we had received from General Clay on this point and was met with hesitation. When I pressed further, the answer came back from our representative among the Big Three that, of course, nothing would be shipped into the American Zone or into any part of Germany until there was an inter-Allied agreement among all four powers. It was an affair for the Allied Supreme Council. As a general refutation, I then produced our letter from the British Army of the Rhine sanctioning our shipping all kinds of materials there.   The President missed the refutation but reacted vigorously.   He pounded the desk that no supplies could be sent anywhere else in Germany until the needs of the American Zone were met first."

Fry's letter continued, quoting himself: "'But, Mr. President, according to your own statement we are not allowed to ship into the American Zone, and won't be for the foreseeable future.   Why then can't we send the clothing which has been accumulated already to the Christians of North Germany (British Zone)?' To that the President said in perplexity, 'You don't think for a moment that we are going to have to wait for the other Allies, do you? Just be patient and we'll have the American Zone open.'"

After more exchange and a reminder that the winter would worsen the suffering, the President finally said, "Don't you worry. We'll have the inter-power agreement and the relief supplies will arrive long before the winter is over."   Fry admitted that "the whole thing sounds as if I am crazy," but he insisted that the conversation was reported accurately, and he left, determined to go out and "build fires."[6]

The National Lutheran Council and its member churches petitioned the President to make it possible for LWR and similar agencies to begin sending relief to Germany, Hungary, Japan, and China.   Among Lutheran individuals who added their voices to the corporate representations, Professor Otto Piper, of Princeton Theological Seminary, sent a carefully reasoned, open letter to the members of the U.S. Congress, calling attention to what he regarded as a constitutional issue. He maintained that millions of American citizens felt "unjustly restricted in their freedom" by the prevailing policy toward former enemies.   He reminded legislators that the First Amendment to the Constitution guarantees the free exercise of religion, and described charity as an essential part of the Christian religion: "We believe that it is our Christian obligation to feed our enemy when he hungers and to act as good Samaritans to everyone who is in need."   Recognizing that others might disagree with this principle, he defended the right of a minority in America to hold such principles and to practice them.[7]

It took two and one-half months of intense suffering in Germany and persistent efforts by Christians in the United States before a solution was reached.   Whatever the actual reasons for the change in policy, President Truman on March 1 issued an official order allowing approved agencies to begin shipping each month a combined total of

2,000 tons of food, clothing, and medicine into the American Zone of Germany, with military space and tonnage allocated on ships.

This action did not end the controversy. The accepted policy of military authorities was to aim for a German diet of 1,550 calories per person per day. Nutrition specialists claimed that 1,550 calories would keep people alive only if they were fairly healthy and were not working. But, after food began to arrive in Germany, some political travelers who ventured only into a few selected areas saw no one actually starving and concluded that no more aid was needed. Lutheran World Relief representatives were appalled by this distortion of reality, and Franklin Fry immediately sent a letter to Lutheran pastors enclosing a refutation for them to take immediately to the editors of their daily newspapers. The statement quoted competent observers offering "incontrovertible evidence of serious food shortages and the imminent threat of starvation among vast numbers of people in areas of distress." The experts included Herbert Hoover, former U.S. president; Joseph T. McNarney, former military governor in Germany; Hans Assmussen, chancellor of the Evangelical Church in Germany; and other church officials. S. C. Michelfelder was quoted reporting, "I stopped along the road where some people were gleaning potatoes after the farmers had dug all they could find. Hundreds of men, women and children were scratching the dusty fields with hoes and their hands, picking up the little potatoes left, even if they were no bigger than marbles.... They told me that they had no potatoes to eat for months and they looked it. There was a haunted look in their faces. The children looked spindly." [8]

Fortunately, President Truman had access to similarly reliable information and he undertook a significant action.

The Marshall Plan

Truman's leadership at this point in history brought about a basic change in U.S. postwar policy. The punitive plan proposed by Secretary of the Treasury Henry Morgenthau would have removed all industry from Germany to neutralize its war potential, reducing the country to an agricultural land. All help was to be minimized to prevent the nation from resuming its role as a world power. It was never adopted, but was being followed until Truman intervened. Coming from Missouri, Truman had observed and experienced some of the traumatic affects of vengeful actions following the Civil War. He resolved to guard against similar results of World War II, and consulted Secretary of State George Marshall. Truman outlined an ambitious plan for foreign aid and, when Marshall inquired about the costs, the President predicted that it would need at least 15 billion dollars. To Marshall's warning that Congress might not support this, Truman replied, "We can save the world with it." Convinced that the plan would go down in history, he wanted Marshall's name associated with it, because of his respect and affection for the general. Marshall protested but, as a good soldier, followed orders and presented the plan in his address at the Harvard Commencement exercises in June, 1947.

Revisionist historians have regarded the Marshall Plan as part of a capitalistic master design, and motives of many supporters were undoubtedly mixed, but Winston Churchill called it "the most unsordid act in history." Truman was certainly aware of its long-term value to the United States, anticipating today's recognition that our well-being is not unrelated to conditions in the rest of the world. To gain support from influential Sam Rayburn he said, "If we let Europe go down the drain, then we're going to have a bad depression in this country. And you and I have both lived through one depression and we don't want to have to live through another one, do we?"[9]

Opportunities provided by this development multiplied the responsibilities for Lutheran World Relief; activity moved into high gear.

Ambassadors for Peace

Lutheran World Relief quickly became one of the major agencies working through CRALOG, the Council of Relief Agencies Licensed to Operate in Germany. There was immediate need for a U.S. representative to supervise the handling and distribution of supplies in Germany, and Carl Schaffnit, then Director of Lutheran Charities in Detroit, Michigan, was recruited for this purpose. He thus became one of a legion of Americans serving as intermediaries between the Lutherans of this country and "family members" abroad. Some were given responsibilities focused on refugees and displaced persons, and Howard Hong, the leader in this enterprise, successfully advocated extending the services to possible resettlement. Lutheran World Relief provided essential supplies for these ministries. The entire resettlement history is thoroughly chronicled in the book, *Open Doors,* by Richard Solberg, who served as senior representative in Germany for the Lutheran World Federation's Department of World Service from 1953 to 1956.[10] Many resettlement workers either already were, or later became, prominent as leaders of American Lutheranism. Since their contributions are recorded by Solberg they will not be repeated here.

There is also, however, an impressive roster of recruits not primarily involved in resettlement but directly connected to Lutheran World Relief. All were accredited to the military government authorities in Berlin and accorded full logistic support by the United States Army, although this did not always simplify travel and communication. Already in 1946 John Scherzer, a pastor from San Antonio, Texas, went to the American Zone in Germany, Frank M. Brown, former army chaplain, to the British Zone, and Owen J. C. Norem, former U.S. Minister to Lithuania, to the French Zone.

These assignments were rotated with some regularity. In 1947 John Scherzer was replaced by Earl K. Rogers, followed by Philip R. Roth. In the French Zone Norem, who had been appointed field director for CRALOG in all of Germany, was succeeded by N. M. Ylvisaker, followed in 1948 by John F. Bauchmann. Norem's CRALOG post was next occupied by Eldon Burke. Carl F. Yaeger went to the British Zone in place of Frank Brown and was succeeded by Carl Mau, who also represented the U.S. National Committee of the LWF in different roles with the Federation in Germany and Geneva. Mau stayed abroad for seven years on these assignments, which were to mark the beginning of a long and distinguished career in global service. Herta Epstein served as LWR and CRALOG representative in Berlin for nine months, followed by John H. Deutschlander and Justine Bodensieck. Her husband, Julius, president of Wartburg Theological Seminary in Dubuque, Iowa, served for six crucial years as Commissioner to Germany for the American Section of the Lutheran World Convention. Carl Schaffnit and John Scherzer were later given assignments in New York benefiting from their overseas experience.[11]

All of these representatives had memorable experiences. Scherzer, despite acknowledging a personal financial loss of $2,500 for the year, wrote to Confer, "I consider it one of the greatest privileges I have experienced and I shall always look upon this year as an opportunity to do my part toward the healing of the world's ills."[12]

Epstein felt strongly that it was essential for LWR to stay in beleaguered Berlin, and she was moved by responses such as a letter from an elderly recipient of food who, with her husband, had been buried under their collapsed house. Their two sons-in-law had been executed under orders from Hitler, and two grandsons had starved to death in Pomerania. They had lost everything, robbed even of their wedding rings, were repeatedly "broken down" and hospitalized from hunger. The woman explained, "I only write this in order to give proof to you that you really gave this gift to somebody who needed it. You have made us poor old people very, very happy.... Please excuse my confused lines but my heart was so full I simply had to write." [13]

Carl Yaeger was the first foreigner to receive, from the Inner Mission Society of Germany, the Wichern Medal, recognizing his "close cooperation and untiring readiness" in the struggle on behalf of the German needy. Carl Mau later was awarded the same medal.[14]

German Bishop Hanns Lilje, who presented the medal to Yaeger, was so impressed by the quality of recruits for the overall ministry to his people that he wrote, "We owe you, the American Lutheran churches, special thanks because you have sent us some of the finest personalities in order to help us." He saw these workers as persons "who, full of understanding, took upon themselves our misery and comforted us by their presence." [15]

They did, indeed, take upon themselves experiences of misery, such as meeting trains arriving in the German border town of Passau, crammed with persons driven from their homes in Poland by Soviet occupying forces. Scherzer was one who did that in the severe winter of 1946-47 and later commented that after being there once, a person did not want to see it again. He explained:

> When the train arrived the doors were unsealed, and the first thing they unloaded was the corpses. They had piled them up against the doors when the cold came in. So they would first unload the dead people, and then next would be the old people and the children and so forth, all of them half frozen to death, and they had not had anything to eat for two or three days, because they had been shoved around from one site to another until they finally arrived at their destination.[16]

Kinship in Service

LWR representatives were fortunate in being able to relate to an effective partner agency in Germany. Immediately after the surrender, leaders of the different German churches, whose relationships with one another had been strained under the Hitler regime, came together and formed the Evangelical Church in Germany (EKID). Michelfelder had sent a letter to the gathering, assuring them of sincere sympathy for their predicament and promising assistance as soon as the armies of occupation allowed it. He called for a reawakening of that "kinship in the faith that once was so strong." Stewart Herman, the only American in attendance, later reported that when the letter was read, "it was like opening the window and letting in a ray of light and a breath of fresh air. This was a note that had not been heard in Germany before. It changed the complexion of the meeting completely. The knowledge that American Lutherans cared made the difference." [17] Other American representatives abroad commented on the prevailing concern of Germans, wondering if they were hated by people in the U. S. Before long, there was additional, concrete evidence that at least some Americans cared, as shipments began arriving.

German church leaders, accustomed to a system under which most of their financial support came from designated taxes, later were so impressed by the generosity of Lutherans from America that they were eager to explore American stewardship practices, and Carl Mau traveled throughout Germany to inform them. LWR thus strengthened partner churches in their capacity to share.[18]

Most of the members in the EKID were independent provincial churches and Lutheran in origin. The founders of this new federation immediately established a relief organization, Evangelisches Hilfswerk, and made provisions for related agencies in each province. In the midst of the prevailing devastation, it was amazing how much aid was undertaken by the Germans themselves. Within five months 20 million Reichsmarks, plus thousands of tons of food and clothing, had been gathered. Much of this came from people who themselves would need help from others. When Allied access to Czechoslovakia, Hungary, and Poland was closed by the Soviets, the Germans persisted in providing whatever assistance was possible. Organized to carry out its mission from within, Evangelisches Hilfswerk was ready to assist LWR and other agencies when channels from abroad were opened. Directed by the dynamic survivor of a concentration camp, Eugen Gerstenmeier, who later became president of the Lower House of the German Parliament, it represented not only Lutherans but all Protestants and worked in close cooperation with the Roman Catholic agency, Caritas, and with the relief organizations of trade unions.

Poorest of the Poor

The relationship with Hilfswerk set a pattern which has prevailed throughout the history of Lutheran World Relief. All actual work overseas is carried on through resident partners, who are in the best position to know local needs and respect local customs and attitudes.

Hilfswerk officials, for example, made recommendations to LWR concerning the allocation among the different military zones in Germany. From the beginning it was agreed that help should go first to the "poorest of the poor," a phrase often used in 1995 but already contained in a 1946 letter from Hilfswerk stating the standards for distribution of American aid in Germany. Assurance was given that "those will get the first help who are in the greatest need without considering their confession and religion, race, party membership or political past. Under special regard are aged people, health-threatened youth, heavily injured vets standing alone, or other people who are of seriously bad health caused by malnutrition. To find these people we must be on permanent look out. Medics and officials of the German Public Health Offices are helping us. Only by careful examination of every single case is it guaranteed that the really suffering get the first incoming relief supplies." [19]

Even saints still sin, according to Lutheran theology, and there were undoubtedly occasional abuses. Some complaints could be traced to misunderstandings, as when it was rumored that relief goods were raffled off at church bazaars. Investigation revealed that at least some of these goods, in accordance with local custom, had been made by women of the local congregations out of remnants of tattered wearing apparel from the overseas bales, and had even been improved by such skills as embroidery until they were actually original creations.

There were also instances where congregations entrusted with food gave priority to members or even prospective members. Generally, however, the principle of allocating strictly on the basis of need was taken very seriously. On one occasion Carl Mau sat with members of a congregational church council who were responsible for distributing ten bags of wheat entrusted to them by Hilfswerk. They debated for almost two hours deciding what to do with those ten bags.[20]

On the surface this policy appeared to run counter to the thrust of appeals to aid the Lutheran family abroad. It was endorsed from the beginning, however, not only because it was a condition of receiving government assistance, but because it encouraged the churches abroad in their own mission of service to all the people in need.

With the opening of access to Germany in March of 1946, and the lifting of monthly tonnage limits in June, LWR naturally began channeling as much as possible to that country. It would be another year before agencies would be allowed to import supplies into Berlin and then the blockade would further complicate shipments into that city. By the end of 1946 almost 1,400 tons of supplies had been shipped to other parts of Germany, most of it clothing and shoes, along with limited shipments of food. LWR adopted a policy to request only foods rich in vitamins, with high caloric content. The initial appeal was confined to canned meats and fish, evaporated, condensed and powdered milk, cocoa, dried soups, and flour. Although these shipments were only a token of what was to be sent later, they brought tremendous encouragement and hope to recipients. In Eugen Gerstenmeier's New Year's greetings to Lutherans of America he wrote:

> Millions of our church members will celebrate the holidays in deep gratitude, for they have experienced in all their poverty and need that the love of Christ is alive in the world beyond our borders and finds its way to us. Every piece of clothing, every can of food that you sent us, became for innumerable people a silent sermon, encouraging them while in despair and giving them new hope.[21]

There was an overwhelming desire, however, for wheat, and churches with large numbers of members farming in the grain belt saw an opportunity to address this need.

Land-based Project

In 1947 Lutheran World Relief and Church World Service began a promotional effort, Christian Rural Overseas Program (CROP), that allowed thousands of Americans to participate very directly in the relief effort. The Lutheran Church—Missouri Synod joined in this venture. Farmers were enlisted in contributing their products to be collected and shipped. Perishable goods were generally exchanged for staples or sold for cash, and corn was usually processed into cereal or syrup. Wheat, however, was gathered in carloads for transport by freighter. The National Catholic Rural Life Conference joined the program a year later. Each agency received what was contributed by its supporters, and non-designated gifts were shared proportionately. A three-person cabinet was put in charge, and the first Lutheran representative was Carl Schaffnit, who was succeeded by Clifford Dahlin.

Much of this effort was carried on through regional CROP committees, which also included representatives of farm organizations. Contributions in different years came from as many as twenty states. Ove Nielsen, whose local involvement in CROP was to lead to many years of service with LWR, remembers how he was recruited as a parish pastor in Montana to help organize a collection of wheat by seeing a film of conditions abroad. Driving home along a road "where wheat was as tall as the side of a horse," he was convinced that, despite the fact that his area had suffered from a complete drought during the two previous years, something should be attempted. Community leaders pitched in and 125 farmers agreed to take their trucks, visit their neighbors, and gather what wheat they could. They brought back 4,320 bushels of wheat that was raised as a mountain of grain on the street outside the courthouse.[22]

Iowa farmers undertook to provide 100 carloads of corn or the cash equivalent. Wisconsin's "Badger Train" collected more than 130 tons of powdered milk and eggs for shipment abroad. An Abraham Lincoln Friendship Train, combining contributions from Lutherans with those from Church World Service, Catholic Relief Services, Mennonites, and others, traveled eastward adding cars until 283 were linked. Nebraska provided 110 cars, Illinois 76, Iowa 45, and the rest came from the Dakotas, Kansas, Colorado, Wyoming, Ohio, Indiana, and Michigan.

A similar effort in the four continental northwest states and Alaska led to the formation of a train to load a Northwest Pacific Christmas Ship which sailed for Bremen and then was reloaded onto a train to travel through parts of Germany unloading the valuable cargo.[23]

People who were not engaged in farming were so attracted to the campaigns that many of them made generous cash contributions as their share in the venture. During the five years of its operation, Lutheran World Relief's share in the project amounted to more than 21 million pounds of supplies and enough additional cash to ship almost 10 million pounds of government-donated surplus commodities.

The whole project had personal meaning at home because it represented the investment of land and labor. In Minnesota a man quit farming for eight weeks to conduct the drive in his county and assisted in collecting commodities valued at $20,000. In Indiana one CROP leader became ill but continued to direct the campaign in five counties from an oxygen tent in a hospital.[24]

Abroad the venture also had special significance, expressed by a German pastor, Bodo Heyne, as he stood on the deck of a freighter accepting on behalf of Evangelische Hilfswerk the 5,000 tons of wheat being unloaded. He said, "Grain and bread are our most important means of subsistence. They are to us holy symbols of our bodily and spiritual life." He went on to say that by sending this wheat Americans "are thus breaking bread for us, and we are, as it were, with them as their guests. Thus is your hand extended to us in the community of Christian thought and action." [25]

There was another important breakthrough in the food situation when, in 1949, Congress passed the Agricultural Assistance Act, making available to approved voluntary agencies "commodities in danger of loss through deterioration or spoilage." This applied to powdered eggs and milk, butter, cheese, and canned beef, and large amounts were soon being shipped by Lutheran World Relief. Already in 1947 the American government had begun reimbursing agencies for shipping costs to West Germany, Austria, and Japan. Since this still did not answer the demand for grains, CROP remained a crucial element in LWR service.

Supplementing the grain from CROP and the government surplus goods, thousands of tons of sugar were shipped, along with soy beans, lard, cereal, rice, raisins, and assorted canned goods. Donations of canned baby food were received from H. J. Heinz and Campbell companies.

Ongoing Need

Lutheran World Relief's services were in full swing by 1950, after five years of intensive effort. Bernard (Bernie as he became known throughout the world) Confer gradually took charge as executive assistant and then as executive director, quickly undertaking the huge load of correspondence along with other duties. He also represented LWR in relationships with many other agencies and became highly respected among colleagues, as indicated by his election to the chairmanship of the American board of the Council of Relief Agencies Licensed for Operation in Germany in February of 1950. The LWR Board of Directors was unchanged from the time of Ralph Long's death in 1948, consisting of Fry as president, Krumbholz as secretary, Telleen as treasurer, Empie and Markel.

To maintain commitment of contributors as the years passed, Empie and Fry regularly emphasized the continuing need. By 1949 congregations could join in thankfulness that destitution was not as all-embracing as four years earlier, but they were also warned that within limited categories it was as poignant and acute as ever. In that year, for example, 1,300,000 persons fled from East Germany into the Western Zone. Such facts caused Empie to write, "Sometimes we get depressed about it. Then we rally to the thought that, in such an hour, God's strength can be made perfect in our weakness. It is for this hour that he has been drawing Lutherans in America together for greater unity, vision, and service." [26]

As peace replaced the wartime years at home, Lutherans did not pull back from their efforts abroad. Shipments included a wide variety of items. Most, by far, were blankets and different types of clothing, both desperately needed. Many resident Germans were wearing the only clothes they possessed, after losing their entire wardrobes in the fires that followed the bombings, or having given their spare clothing to fellow citizens who had lost everything. Refugees came wearing only tattered rags and bandaged feet. [27]

Carl Schaffnit secured donations of toweling, hosiery, flannel, yarn, shoe laces, yard goods, and twine from textile manufacturers in North Carolina, and John Bauchmann later made a similar appeal. Shoes, both new and repaired, were sent in great quantities. There was even a purchase of 100,000 pairs of surplus Army half-soles, and shoe repair equipment was in great demand. The list of supplies also included soap, seed, candles, writing equipment, cooking equipment, sheeting, tools, cotton, yarn, and twine.

Medicines, especially insulin, penicillin, and cod liver oil, were sent regularly. A Medical-Surgical Relief Committee, representing a number of voluntary agencies, was formed to solicit drugs from the manufacturers. It was later replaced by a more efficient agency, the Interchurch Medical Assistance Program, for which Ove Nielsen became one of five incorporators.

Two other extremely useful items were being created by women of the churches: layettes and Kiddies Kits. The layettes contained everything needed to care for a newborn baby, and a typical Kiddies Kit contained personal items such as washcloth, soap, comb, tooth brush and paste, along with writing tablet, pencils, and a chocolate bar.

For many years Carl F. Lorey, assistant administrative secretary, handled the complex task of arranging for all of LWR's shipping. Various warehouses were used in Pennsylvania, California, Washington, Minnesota, Indiana, and Maryland. Because of the fluctuating volume it was more economical to rent from private agencies or at least to share such facilities, so LWR contracted with different agencies, including Church World Service, Church of the Brethren, and at one time the Good Samaritan Society of Southern California.

Focus Still on Lutheran Family

During the first five years of LWR work, more than 80% of all shipments went to Germany, with most of the rest going to other countries of western Europe. Japan and the Middle East did receive substantial amounts, with Brazil and China also among the recipients.

This meant that there was still an emphasis on serving the Lutheran family. Even outside Germany, contact was established through minority churches or Lutheran missions. Relief work in the West Bank of Jordan, among refugees displaced in the 1948 creation of the state of Israel, was launched through the efforts of Edwin Moll, who had represented the Lutheran World Federation in Jerusalem from before the partition of Palestine. Moll was widely acquainted throughout Jordan and was even a western confidant of King Abdullah, grandfather of King Hussein.[28] In addition to those crowded into the West Bank, almost a million people left Palestine with the establishment of the Israeli government and fled to neighboring countries already impoverished. The Lutheran World Federation began an extensive ministry of relief and medical services, to which LWR has made significant contributions. This, in fact, is the one area where LWR relief work as such has been continuous for nearly fifty years, and where there has been no real resolution of poverty.

Moll was frustrated by the inability to move toward permanent solutions, attributing this impasse to "hard-hearted, coldly calculating politicians," and he anticipated LWR's future move toward development. In 1949 he proposed that LWR support the establishment of clothing and shoe manufacturing operations, maintaining that employment for Palestinians was essential, but LWR was not ready for such a step.[29]

It was true that all aid was to be distributed on the basis of need and without regard for religious affiliation, but it was also true that, since such a high percentage of people in most of the areas served were Lutherans, they would be helped under this agreement. Krumbholz did not apologize for the special family concerns. He said, "While this appeal is in the interest of all needy peoples, without discrimination, we are, nevertheless, aware of our responsibility for the lives and welfare of Europe's more than 60 million Lutherans. We have no right to expect others to assume this tremendous burden."[30]

Extended Need, Expanded Partnership

When the founders of Lutheran World Relief held their first conversations about forming a new agency, they did not intend it to be permanent. Despite the enormity of the task they were undertaking, they thought that it could be accomplished within a few years, and Europe would be sufficiently restored to address its own needs. When Krumbholz employed Confer, it was with the understanding that the position would probably last for three years, after which Krumbholz should be able to locate a social agency where Confer might serve as administrator. Since Confer wanted time to consider his future, such an interim assignment appealed to him. As late as January, 1950, in answering a question about the future of LWR, Confer could only say, "It appears certain that it will go on a couple more years." [1]

By then, however, all connected with Lutheran World Relief realized that they were involved in something far greater than they had anticipated. Japan's economy was sufficiently viable by 1954 that relief to that country could be discontinued, but the situation elsewhere was still critical. In 1950 Lutheran World Relief sent more goods to Germany than any other voluntary agency associated with the Council of Relief Agencies Licensed for Operation in Germany; LWR's shipments accounted for more than one third of CRALOG's total. Restoring self-sufficiency to Germany would take longer than expected, primarily because of the continuing flow of refugees and displaced persons from Soviet-dominated countries.

Although American contributions were so essential in the immediate postwar years, there was a clear understanding within LWR that this was not to lead to U.S. domination of relief efforts. From the beginning LWR officials had a vision of a global partnership where resources would be placed "on the table" for Lutherans of the world to decide how best to use them. It can be said that Americans gave birth to LWF's service programs, beginning with S. C. Michelfelder's initial leadership. Paul Empie, supported by Bernard Confer, led in the formation of the LWF Department of World Service, and another American, Henry Whiting, became its first director. All of them realized that LWR's effectiveness would be multiplied by close ties with Lutherans throughout the world.

An obvious benefit from this international relationship was the eventual availability of greatly increased resources for service. It wasn't long before Swedes began participating, and soon even the Germans made commitments. Gradually American contributions to the work of the Lutheran World Federation became only a fraction of the support from the German and north European churches.

Lutheran World Relief continued for years to be funded principally by money raised through Lutheran World Action, the appeal begun in 1940 by the National Lutheran Council to finance many activities. By 1958 LWA total receipts had reached 50 million dollars, of which more than 30 million had been allocated to the Lutheran World Federation, primarily for the departments of World Service and World Mission. In the U.S. the Bureau of Service to Military Personnel had received more than five million, and Lutheran Refugee Service and Lutheran World Relief had been granted more than two and one-half million each.[2] By the late fifties LWR, with less than $250,000 per year from its parent agency, was shipping millions of dollars worth of supplies abroad each year. After large government surplus amounts became available, the annual figure averaged more than 14 million dollars from 1956 through 1959.

Lutheran World Action was always well organized nationally, telling its story through promotional materials supplied to all congregations of National Lutheran Council church bodies. Regional directors operated on synodical, district, conference, and circuit levels. Colorful handbooks and occasional films were produced. Special bulletins were mailed monthly to pastors. The News Bureau of the National Lutheran Council fed releases to the public media; the NLC magazine, the *National Lutheran*, along with periodicals of the church bodies, regularly carried articles about relief efforts. Inspirational speakers addressed rallies throughout the country. Paul Empie, one of the most active of these, once recalled how he "used to 'stump' the country in 30-day trips, going down the East Coast and through Texas and up through California, speaking to pastors and laymen morning, afternoon and evening—3½ hours in the morning, luncheon meetings, 3½ hours in the afternoon, and a big mass rally at night."[3] He spoke to tens of thousands of people, and the process of appealing for gifts also served the important purpose of educating members concerning global needs and alerting them to the nature of Christian responsibility toward neighbors.

The title, Lutheran World Action, under the symbol of the cross and the arm, "Love's Working Arm," became more recognizable than

the names of the National Lutheran Council, the Lutheran World
Federation, or even Lutheran World Relief. In 1958 Lutheran World
Relief adopted as its emblem LWA's arm and cross, within outlines of
the heart and five-petaled rose seal of Martin Luther, with "LWR"
printed in bold letters below. It was later replaced by a simpler
emblem with a cross and plant leaves superimposed on a globe.

Strengthened Cooperation

To cope with the increasingly complex task of addressing global
needs, Lutheran World Relief was strengthened in the fifties by the
decision of The Lutheran Church—Missouri Synod to become a full
partner.

The LCMS had been active on its own in relief efforts. In
response to the devastation from World War I, a General Board of
Relief had been formed in 1914. World War II prompted the establishment of a new body, the National Advisory Planning Council,
coordinating efforts of the Lutheran Laymen's League, the Walther
League, the Lutheran Women's Missionary League, and other boards
and commissions of the Synod. Members responded generously to
pleas for help. In 1946, for example, more than two and one-half
million dollars were contributed. In 1950 a Department of Social
Welfare was also established.[4]

One LCMS approach to relief was contrary to an LWR policy.
Through a "Units for Europe" program, contributions were solicited for
the mailing of packets costing $7.50 each and containing such items as
food, clothing, and medicine. The project had one advantage over
LWR's more economical practice of shipping only in bulk: it emphasized the personal element in relief ministry and therefore had special
appeal to potential contributors. LCMS also worked more closely with
sister congregations abroad, not being connected with either the
Lutheran World Federation or the World Council of Churches.

On all major relief issues, however, there was agreement between
the two global agencies. There had always been instances of cooperation, as when some Missouri shipments had been channeled through
LWR, with costs borne by LCMS. Joint efforts were extended through
participation by both agencies in the Christian Rural Overseas Program.
CROP provided a significant amount of the food shipped by Lutherans
in the late forties and early fifties, but the program's success was
threatened by a bureaucratic weevil. Overhead expenses had escalated

until LWR policy makers decided in 1952 that Lutheran World Relief should withdraw from further participation, and LCMS agreed. The Roman Catholics also withdrew and Church World Service, recognizing that changes were necessary, was permitted to retain the name and reshape the agency to make it function more responsibly. (Years later Lutheran congregations were again encouraged to participate in the reorganized CROP, with LWR again receiving designated proceeds from event participants.)

Lutherans decided to launch their own replacement for CROP and a new organization was formed, with John Scherzer as its first director. He was succeeded by Ove Nielsen, who was assisted by an LCMS pastor, Oscar Decker. When the name, All-Lutheran Food Appeal, was adopted, it had special meaning for Lutherans because the new organization, including LCMS, represented more Lutherans than ever before. Unwittingly, however, it offended some others to whom it indicated that Lutherans were abandoning their ecumenical effort and excluding non-Lutherans from joining in relief efforts.[5] The organization was discontinued when government surplus food became available in great quantities, but during its three years of operation it received food gifts for overseas relief worth more than $1,500,000. Director Nielsen then became executive assistant to Bernard Confer, where he served with distinction for 23 years.

Meanwhile, The Lutheran Church—Missouri Synod had also been participating with the National Lutheran Council in work such as Lutheran Service Centers and services to prisoners of war. In 1953 LCMS changed the name of its General Relief Board to Board of World Relief, with Werner Kuntz as executive secretary and Edwin A. Nerger as chairperson. Oswald C. J. Hoffman, then public relations director of LCMS, suggested to President John Behnken that it might be time for a closer relationship with Lutheran World Relief, since LCMS was only contributing for services provided by LWR without sharing in costs of the regular budget, and without much voice in policy-making. Behnken agreed, and after Kuntz and Nerger conferred with Bernard Confer and Franklin Fry, they were convinced that more active cooperation between LCMS and LWR was in everyone's best interests.

Both Kuntz and Nerger first began attending LWR Directors' meetings on a consultative basis. Then, in 1955, the relationship was formalized when they were elected to membership on the LWR Board.[6] Within Missouri it was understood that joint ministry "in deed" did not involve compromise over theological convictions concerning authenticity of ministry "in Word."

Kuntz and Confer worked closely together in administrative matters, and carried on a continuous correspondence reflecting mutual respect and friendship. Nerger, as a pastor from a large congregation in Fort Wayne, brought to the board an important perspective from his parish experience, and served as a director for 30 years, many of them as secretary. In this same period there were other changes in the board. In 1954, Frederick Telleen, one of the original incorporators, resigned because of poor health and was replaced by Sigurd J. Arnesen, who was replaced in 1959 by Elmer S. Hjortland. Harold Osterman was added in 1954 but lived only until 1958, when he was replaced by Kenneth Priebe. Clarence Krumbholz died in 1956 and was replaced by Henry J. Whiting.

Since 1955, LCMS has been a full participant in LWR, eventually contributing to a proportionate share of administrative costs as well as to shipping costs for projects of its own Board of World Relief. In 1958 two representatives of the Evangelical Joint Synod of Wisconsin and Other States (later named Wisconsin Evangelical Lutheran Synod) began attending meetings of the LWR Board as consultants, and this relationship has continued through the years, with Wisconsin participating in certain projects and contributing on a voluntary basis.

The End of the Beginning

The task which had been addressed separately by LCMS and the churches of the National Lutheran Council was now being undertaken with combined resources through Lutheran World Relief. And it was still a formidable one. Not until the end of 1959 would West German Protestants give notice that, within the next year, they would no longer need shipments from abroad but would be able by themselves to "assume the task of material assistance." By then, they said, even the needs of East Germans in the Soviet Zone would be the special task of the churches in the West.[7] Meanwhile Germans in the West were finding ways to send into East Germany packages of food, some of which had been supplied by LWR.

Throughout the fifties LWR would have a major involvement in completing the task of alleviating the suffering from World War II in Europe, especially in Germany. The need for clothing and blankets continued to be critical. In 1952 one thousand refugees per day were pouring into West Berlin, where 300,000 residents were without work.

Many of the newcomers arrived without any baggage. Five years later, during 1957, more than 300,000 refugees were still estimated to have crossed the border somewhere from the East Zone.

Lutherans showed initiative in responding to the LWR clothing appeal. Charles A. Puls, a Wisconsin pastor, spent $18.50 for three-cent stamps to enlist other pastors and laypersons in spearheading a concentrated campaign that produced seven and one-half carloads of used clothing from 10 centers scattered throughout the state. University students were enlisted, and even young children, during their traditional "trick or treat" visits at Halloween, asked for clothing instead of candy. Puls publicized the project in a speech, "They Are Cold," on a Madison radio station, and newspapers covered the effort with photos and even editorials.[8]

LCMS participation had an immediate impact on LWR shipments of clothing and blankets. In many areas, congregations of NLC bodies and of LCMS worked together to provide carload lots. Women of all the church bodies contributed generously in money and labor. It was soon discovered that handmade quilts would serve important purposes, and women's organizations throughout the country began assembling groups to meet regularly and participate actively in a creative ministry of service.

At first the quilts were needed primarily for emergencies in bitter north European climates, so the rougher and thicker the materials, the more useful the product. Old winter coats were sometimes dismantled and remade into heavy quilts. A story making the rounds among quilters tells of one woman's experience in coming to a sewing session wearing a thoroughly worn coat which she put aside on arrival but never found again because it had been used in the quilting process. Assumed to be apocryphal, the tale became credible when the accidental contributor was identified as Dagny Schiotz, widow of Fredrik A. Schiotz, loyal LWR supporter as president of member churches and the LWF.[9] Since those early years, most quilts are made from lighter materials and serve different but equally important purposes. In the desert, for example, they can be used by day as shelters from the sun, and at night may become ground cloths to protect against the cold sand.

Germany was still in need of food throughout the fifties. In 1958, for example, food sent to Hilfswerk by LWR was being distributed to 30,000 children in schools, 102,000 residents of institutions, and 399,000 in family units. By that time Eugene Ries and Frederick Otto, staff members of the Lutheran World Federation, represented LWR in

Germany.[10] Just as the Austrian economy had begun to revive, events in Hungary brought a new stream of refugees across that border.

The need was finally addressed, however, by substantial government assistance. The modest program begun in 1949 and 1950 was suspended early in 1951, and the real surge in food shipments did not begin until ten years after the devastation had become apparent, and after needs elsewhere exceeded the needs in Germany. In 1954 Congress adopted Public Law 480, the "Agricultural Trade and Assistance Act," later known as "Food for Peace," authorizing the donation of commodities deemed in surplus. These first included powdered milk, butter, butter oil, cheese, cottonseed oil, and shortening, but in 1955 Ezra Taft Benson, Secretary of Agriculture, pressured by church agencies, began releasing some of the vast surplus of grain.[11] Although a belated outcome of the Marshall Plan, Food for Peace owed its existence to the policy established by Truman and Marshall.

Lutheran World Relief's first shipments under the new provisions sailed in the second quarter of 1956. They included 68 carloads or more than five million pounds of flour, rice, beans, and wheat. This development allowed LWR shipments of food to increase steadily. From 17 million pounds in 1954 the figure reached 122 million in 1959, with flour ordinarily accounting for half of the tonnage. The U.S. government also reimbursed LWR for most costs of ocean freight. During the fifties LWR shipped to Germany alone more than 132 million pounds of supplies, valued at more than 35 million dollars. Until 1955 Germany received the major portion of LWR shipments, after which the tonnage was reduced gradually until it was terminated at the end of the decade. One chapter in LWR's history had ended, but it was only the end of the beginning.

Lutheran WORLD Relief

Within a decade of Lutheran World Relief's founding, the outlook was radically different from what had been anticipated in 1945 and 1946. As the tragic situation in Europe gradually improved, the pressing needs of people in other lands could not be disregarded. LWR confronted a range of challenges that were old in some respects, new in others. It was time for the first of a number of periodic self-examinations.

By the middle of the fifties, major allotments of LWR supplies were going outside western Europe to Yugoslavia, Palestine, Syria, Korea, Taiwan, Hong Kong, and India. Smaller amounts soon began to go annually to countries suffering from droughts, hurricanes, and floods. By 1960, 36 countries had received one or more shipments since LWR's beginning. Many of those countries, such as Italy and France, were home to Lutheran minorities. Others, like India, were the location of Lutheran missionary efforts. In fact, however, LWR was already reaching far beyond the boundaries of the Lutheran family.

There were 150,000 Lutherans in Yugoslavia in 1946. Louis Sanjek, a Croatian Lutheran pastor on the staff of the National Lutheran Council, gathered the names of all the pastors in that country and began supplying them with packages from the stocks of LWR. In most of the Soviet-dominated countries, relief from American agencies was shut off soon after the war, but when Marshal Tito broke with the Kremlin, the way was opened for a remarkable relationship. Tito's administration was notably authoritarian, as evidenced in reverse by the failure of his successors to hold together the factions of his artificially created nation, and he refused access to his country for most agencies. But he was impressed by LWR's record elsewhere, its assurance to serve all without distinction, and its willingness to work through the Yugoslavian Red Cross. Beginning in 1950, therefore, LWR was permitted to send large shipments of clothing and food, concentrated on schools. During the following years Yugoslavia suffered a series of disasters, including an earthquake, floods, and prolonged drought, resulting in Yugoslavia receiving, in a number of years, the largest total relief shipment sent anywhere by LWR.

In 1957 Lutheran World Relief and Church World Service together
were providing a meal which constituted both breakfast and lunch each
school day in 14,000 public schools for 1,800,000 students, approximately three-fourths of all Yugoslav children under the age of thirteen.
Corn meal, powdered milk, cheese and flour were sent to the schools,
where townspeople set up kitchens to prepare the meals. A study later
revealed that the food contributed to significant changes in the health
of the children. Malnourishment was no longer apparent; children were
growing at a normal rate; anemia decreased (supported by hemoglobin
tests); mouth diseases were eliminated. Children became more regular
in attendance, were more alert, and evidenced improvement in hygienic
habits.[1]

LWR also sent many tons of clothing to Yugoslavia. When the
country later became self-sufficient and no more regular assistance was
needed, Tito authorized a state dinner in New York, during which a
government representative praised Lutheran World Relief, saying,
"We're not Christians but we have always respected you because you
have always practiced what you preached. You said you were there to
help people in the name of your Jesus, and that's what you did." [2]

Relief to the Palestinians also had LWR priority in the fifties.
During a 33-month period between 1950 and 1953 Lutheran World
Relief headed the list of American voluntary agencies aiding Arab
refugees in the Middle East with used clothing shipments. More than
1,500,000 pounds were sent by LWR during that time, some of it being
channeled through Jordan and Syria.[3]

In 1958 Lutheran women's groups from all of the LWR
participating churches began a new program with the distinctive
purpose to provide "Arab-fashion" clothing for Arab refugee children.
It was titled the "Dorcas Project," appropriately named for the woman
of old Joppa who made coats and garments for the poor, as reported in
the book of Acts. Garments cut from patterns made in Jordan were
sewed together by American women. The program was designed to
help children entering school to have a greater sense of dignity and
security than they were likely to have experienced in the refugee
camps. For many children the garments would be their first new
clothing. Women's organizations bought packages costing $25 and
containing pre-cut materials for 12 girls' dresses and 12 boys' shirts
and short pants. Sewing instructions were included in each unit. More
than 60,000 garments were assembled during the first year.

The situation in Yugoslavia and Palestine was typical, in a way,
of what happened in other places. A service begun because of the

presence of Lutherans in an area was extended immediately to all in need. The recipients soon could be described as "strangers," some of whom were undoubtedly unsympathetic to American policies or even Christian beliefs. There was some fear that donors might question the direction being taken, but Edwin Nerger remembers the obvious scriptural answers cited by board members: "If you do good to those who do good to you, what credit is that to you?" and "If your enemy is hungry, feed him; if he is thirsty, give him drink."

Today we talk about the "extended family," by which we mean relatives beyond parents and children, but the biblical view of family includes "all God's children." And Lutheran World Relief soon extended its mission of mercy to lands where previous Lutheran presence, if any, had been very limited. The agency's Annual Report for 1956 began with the statement, "The Christian Church owes a special ministry to the neglected, the overlooked, the anonymous needy, and those upon whom the forces of destruction and misery have descended." During that year Bernard Confer and Werner Kuntz had visited Korea, Hong Kong, Taiwan, India, Jordan, Syria, and Germany to study needs and meet with local people prepared to implement the distribution of relief supplies. As a result, increased emphasis was directed to Asia.

The Neediest

If food and clothing were to be distributed within a German village strictly on the basis of need, could the same priority be applied to the world? Should relief go first to the very poorest nations? In principle, the concept made sense; applying it to actual situations involved complications. In Europe recovery was facilitated by the presence of leaders and structures that were not easily identified in other parts of the world. Funds from Lutherans in America were not unlimited; how far could they be stretched? All such questions would be addressed by the directors within a few years, but in the fifties the needs were so pressing that actions were taken before clear answers could be formulated.

By the end of the fifties, four locations in Asia were receiving from Lutheran World Relief more shipments than any country except Yugoslavia. Three of these were suffering from the effects of World War II: Hong Kong, Taiwan, and Korea.

In Hong Kong the spectacular "Pearl of the Orient" was disfigured by a condition of squalor and desperation. Thousands of refugees came each month from mainland China, adding to a congestion of more than half a million people in urgent need. Housing projects built by the government could not keep pace with the flow, and families were living on sidewalks, between buildings, in staircases, on roof tops, and especially in their scrap wood and cardboard squatter huts on open hillsides above the city. They needed clothing, food, and medical help. Many had tuberculosis. LWR was sending food, clothing, and medicines on a regular basis to groups numbering between 50,000 and 80,000. Distribution was handled by the Department of World Service of the Lutheran World Federation.

Taiwan presented a contrast between affluence and poverty. The slopes and valleys were so productive that sugar and rice were being exported while more than a million people were seriously undernourished and ill-clad. Many of them were refugees from mainland China, some of them having come to Taiwan by way of Hong Kong.

Tensions were high between the Taiwanese and the dominant mainlanders. Despite a vast flow of military and economic aid from the United States, little reached the most needy people, for some of whom, at least, LWR provided clothing, supplementary food, and medicine. At the request of Taiwan Church World Service, the agency that handled distribution for LWR, some supplies were diverted to Quemoy, the island located only a few miles from mainland China.

During the Korean conflict LWR became a founding member of American Relief for Korea (ARK), although there were no Lutheran congregations in the land. As soon as government permission was granted, in 1951, shipments of supplies began and were continued long after the war's end because of the prevailing needs. South Korea is little more than twice as large as Denmark but had more than five times as many inhabitants; 70% of the land was unfit to till without irrigation. Estimates of the number of persons needing relief in the mid-fifties ranged from half a million to two million. Of this number LWR supplied food on a regular basis to approximately 100,000 people.

Distribution of supplies in Korea was provided, as usual, by a local agency, in this case Korean Church World Service. Unfortunately, serious problems arose in the administration of the program. In the climate of wartime, government corruption had become rampant and standards of morality were undermined. To keep vehicles moving, bribes seemed to be needed. There was evidence that some supplies donated by the U.S. were appearing on the black market. Alerted to the situation by Hugh Farley, a conscientious executive on the staff of the International Cooperation Administration, Lutheran World Relief took action by sending James P. Claypool to Korea to investigate the situation. While taking charge of the mass distribution he verified some abuses, recommended ways to correct them, and was enlisted to serve for three years, until August, 1958, as director of Korean Church World Service. He worked closely with a Korean general manager, preserving the relationship between overseas service and indigenous responsibility.[4]

In all three locations, Hong Kong, Taiwan, and Korea, plus the Palestinian areas, there was a special demand for layettes. In a letter addressed to women of the Lutheran churches in the U.S., Ove Nielsen identified those countries as places where thousands of children were born each day without "swaddling clothes." He wrote, "Of all the things sent overseas for the needy by Lutheran World Relief, none is more sought after than the layette." Lutheran women contributed generously, as they have continued to respond in the years since then.

India was another Asian nation beginning to receive substantial aid from Lutheran World Relief in the fifties, but in that case the needs came less from military devastation or dislocation than from general desolation. Several million refugees did come out of East Pakistan after India was partitioned in 1947, but the resulting conditions differed from earlier ones in degree rather than in kind.

Whole regions of famine resulting from drought or floods have been common in India. Poverty has been prevalent. In the mid-fifties two and one-half million people had tuberculosis; five hundred thousand died annually from the disease. In Calcutta the hungry poor could be seen by the thousands making their hard beds on public pavements, railroad platforms, and under bridges. The government was working to improve food production but it was not enough to keep pace with the increase in population. It was not until the next decade that the government was more successful in addressing the need for birth control. By 1959 LWR was sending supplementary food for more than 180,000 people, channeled through the National Christian Council of India to schools, welfare institutions, and churches. John J. Steinhoff, a Lutheran Church—Missouri Synod missionary, was the LWR representative in India.

Lutheran World Relief did not begin active, continuing service in Africa and Latin America until the end of the fifties, by which time the concept of relief had been broadened beyond immediate, temporary assistance.

Geared for Disaster Response

Lutheran World Relief sent materials during the fifties to a number of countries not yet mentioned, but this was generally in response to a sudden catastrophe. In the process another distinctive function for LWR was recognized. Equipped to minister to a continuing need in a particular country, LWR was uniquely prepared to respond to a sudden disaster in that country or even in a neighboring land. Thus in 1954, when a flood disaster in Baghdad left a half million people homeless and virtually isolated, LWR was able to contribute 20 tons of clothing and food to the first shipment of supplies to reach Iraq's capital city. The waters of the Tigris and Euphrates rivers, swollen by rains and melting snow from the mountains of eastern Turkey and northern Iraq, had made Baghdad appear to be an island, with the farmland north and east of the city transformed into a lake covering 150 to 200 square miles. The LWR supplies came from stocks in Beirut and Jerusalem, and included milk and cheese from U.S. surplus commodities.[5]

Help was provided to deal with floods and typhoons in Hong Kong, Korea, and Taiwan from LWR supplies already available in those lands. In 1959 Japan was hit by Typhoon Vera, killing 4,000, injuring 850,000, and leaving more than a million people homeless. Three days after Lutheran World Relief in New York received an urgent request to help victims, 24,512 pounds of clothing and bedding arrived in the stricken country. Although there had been no LWR relief to Japan for a number of years, the speedy reply to the disaster call was made possible by diverting to Japan a shipment of relief goods bound for Korea.[6] Madagascar and Brazil were among other countries receiving some form of assistance, either supplies or funds. In many of these emergencies, cooperation with the Lutheran World Federation and the World Council of Churches was very important.

Relations With Other Governments

To minister to the people of so many nations, Lutheran World Relief also entered into different relationships with various governments. Generally, the service was welcomed. Franklin Clark Fry, Bernard Confer, and Carl Mau were honored by the Federal Republic of Germany in appreciation for their roles in LWR and in the Council of Relief Agencies Licensed for Operation in Germany. Fry was awarded the Grand Cross of the Order of Merit in 1953 and both Confer and Mau received the Commander's Cross of the Order of

Merit in 1957. Fry and Confer were also presented with honorary citizenship in the Republic of Korea in 1953. In 1958 Yugoslavia honored Confer and Werner Kuntz by conferring upon them the Gold Medal of the Yugoslav Red Cross.[7]

Not all contacts with governments abroad were so amicable. In Poland, where there had been 200,000 Lutherans before the war and where LWR had been sending clothing and food annually from 1946 to 1951, restrictions were imposed to prevent this contact with the West until 1958, when "a more relaxed attitude" on the part of the Polish government allowed relief shipments to be resumed. Similar restrictions generally prevailed in other countries dominated by the Soviet Union: Czechoslovakia, Rumania, Estonia, Latvia, and, of course, East Germany.[8]

In 1958 the Hungarian government suspended LWR shipments, evidently because officials of the Lutheran World Federation had criticized the State's action forcing a bishop to resign and replacing him with one more friendly to the government. Presumed U.S. influence on LWR actions could be interpreted to reflect anti-communist policy to the extent that advocates of socialism and citizens in socialist countries would be handicapped by any contact with the agency.[9]

In Taiwan Lutheran World Relief participated with other voluntary agencies in approaching government officials to investigate and eliminate a particular evil prevailing on the island. Unwanted daughters were being sold to anyone who wanted them for whatever purpose. Some became household servants, many were forced into hard manual labor such as work in coal mines, and others were being recruited as teahouse waitresses or prostitutes. Both the churches in the country and the government were called upon for concerted action to wipe out the practice.[10] Ministry in places like Taiwan and Korea, where peace remained fragile, required special discretion on the part of LWR representatives.

Church and State Questions

As valuable as the U.S. government support for overseas relief proved to be, it also raised questions concerning the relationship between church and state. When LWR representatives saw at firsthand pressing needs that could be addressed by the U.S. government, it was natural to lobby the administration and Congress to take action, as when fats and oils were needed to supplement other commodities for the sake of improved diets among the hungry people abroad. Once when the House had voted to reduce an appropriation for shipping costs to assist voluntary agencies in transporting surplus food abroad, Hubert Humphrey was enlisted to lead the Senate in restoring the original figure. Encouraged by his strongly Lutheran constituency in Minnesota, Humphrey made the valid point that the U.S., working through voluntary agencies, was getting much more for its investment than if the money were spent directly by a government agency. He quoted President Eisenhower's statement in a message to Congress, stressing that "one of the unique, least expensive, and most fruitful aspects of the mutual security program is the participation, largely in humanitarian projects, of 47 voluntary programs representing millions of our citizens." [11]

More basic issues were also addressed by LWR leadership. Early in the fifties voluntary agencies detected a shift in emphasis of U.S. foreign aid policy from economic recovery to rearmament, threatening reimbursement of ocean freight expense for relief shipments to certain countries. A new provision in the Mutual Security Act restricted economic assistance for foreign nations "to projects specifically in the interests of the security of the United States." This indicated such a departure from unselfish and humanitarian objectives that it seemed to be incompatible with the basic operating principles of relief agencies. Bernard Confer issued a statement on behalf of Lutheran World Relief, pointing to the millions of war victims still destitute. He said, "We are convinced that the humanitarian concern of the American people ought to be reflected in the policies of our government," adding that "in efforts to increase the well-being of people in the long run lay the firmest foundation for goodwill and peace among the nations." [12] Resolutions critical of the threatened shift were adopted by the governing bodies of both LWR and the National Lutheran Council. A standoff was averted when new congressional legislation was enacted transferring the reimbursement of shipping costs to the State Department and tying such reimbursement to the more unselfish objectives of the original Marshall Plan.

Already in 1952 Confer was also looking beyond the wartime emergency and calling on the government to be prepared to support a program of technical assistance to help people in the so-called underdeveloped areas of the world to develop their resources and mold their own future.

In relating to the U.S. government, LWR leaders were aware from the beginning of possible conflicts with the nature of their ministry. Too close an association with government agencies could make

Lutheran World Relief appear to be an instrument of the United States, thereby compromising its character in the eyes of recipients abroad. Paul Empie expressed this dilemma in testifying on behalf of LWR before the Foreign Relations Committee in 1959. The U.S. had sold grain to some countries for foreign currency to be retained in those countries as "counterpart" funds; there was now a proposal that those funds be released to U.S. voluntary agencies for their use, possibly even for paying part of their operating costs. Empie questioned the wisdom of such an action, fearing that it would tend to shift the burden of support of an agency's program from the gifts of its constituency to contributions from government. He was convinced that "funds from government, whether in the form of counterpart foreign currencies or dollars, for the purpose of employing staff, renting office space, and meeting other administrative requirements abroad, no matter how well safeguarded by the wording of legislation," could not fail to be construed as a direct subsidy to the agency. He also contended that the use of the special counterpart funds for technical assistance or educational projects might seem to make the voluntary agency come too close to being an agent of the government.[13]

Confronting Basic Issues

From its beginning, Lutheran World Relief had been so busy doing the work it was clearly called to do, that there had been little time to question the direction it was taking. The pioneers must have been guided by the traditional prayer: "Lord God, you have called your servants to ventures of which we cannot see the ending, by paths as yet untrodden, through perils unknown. Give us faith to go out with good courage, not knowing where we go, but only that your hand is leading us and your love supporting us; through Jesus Christ, our Lord."

Now more attention had to be given to the rationale under an enterprise steadily growing in its extent and complexity. Relations with government did not constitute the only perplexing question. Decisions had to be made concerning LWR's cooperation with other voluntary agencies in the field. LWR's role as a Lutheran agency in a time of ecumenical emphasis was under consideration. Pervading everything else was the realization that LWR had reached so far beyond its original goal of ministering temporarily to its Lutheran family that it was now attempting to serve the endemic needs of an extended family that included all of humanity. Was this what was expected by the constituency? Was it truly the will of God? Was it wise stewardship?

Would contributors continue to support such a diversified and unending effort? Should Christian service to physical needs be extended without a clear connection to spiritual mission?

Staff and board members were not unanimous in their answers to such questions, and there was even doubt as to whether there were wholly right or wrong answers to be given. In 1959, therefore, a policy committee was appointed to study the questions and submit recommendations to the board. It was 1961 before the recommendations were ready for consideration, leading the way into a new decade. Meanwhile, there was no doubt that Lutheran World Relief was here to stay.

A Continuing Purpose

By the end of the fifties it was apparent that a relief agency representing Lutherans in the U.S. could serve a number of vital, continuing functions. LWR could work through special channels for generating support from a large number of committed believers. Separately incorporated, LWR could have access to government resources and could act quickly without waiting for decisions from the ecclesiastical decision-making process. Happily, LWR had also established its integrity to the point where its actions were respected and approved by church authorities. The global connection with other Lutheran and Protestant communions provided means for direct, reliable contact with people all over the world, especially important in crisis situations. Lutheran World Relief's concentration on overseas relief, to the virtual exclusion of domestic needs, did raise some questions, but experience indicated that this was also a plus, and it became an adopted policy. It allowed LWR's limited resources and staff to be focused for effectiveness. Existing American agencies could be relied upon to deal with domestic affairs. The only exceptions have been times when supplies stored in LWR warehousing could be used in disastrous situations, such as floods or hurricanes, in the United States.

Lutheran World Relief had changed from the modest agency established in 1945. It would continue to change and grow in response to needs and opportunities that could barely be imagined in 1959.

BREMEN IN 1945, the Germany where U.S. Lutherans saw their task as feeding, clothing and housing erstwhile enemies.

ONE IN FIVE of the world's Lutherans was a refugee, mostly in central Europe, after World War II.

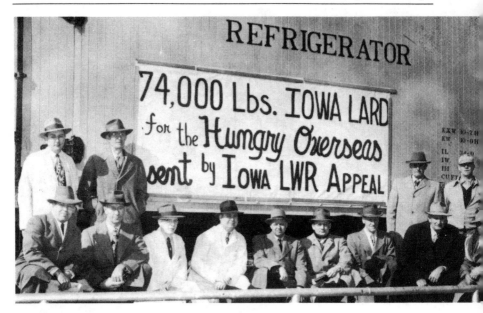

CORNBELT COMPASSION mobilized for the needy in Europe and, after LWR helped change U.S. policy, in Germany itself.

A GERMAN PASTOR said of LWR aid that Americans "are thus breaking bread for us and we are with them as guests" (p. 33).

THE VISION stretched in the 1950s. In Hong Kong LWR aid reached up to 80,000 mainland Chinese refugees each month (p. 46).

PALESTINE has received aid for nearly all of LWR's 50 years. As elsewhere, help reached far beyond any local Lutheran presence (p.35).

YUGOSLAVIA'S Marshal Tito (center) meets Paul Empie (left) and Franklin Clark Fry (right), leaders in LWR's early years.

RALPH LONG (seated), whose vision and initiative guided the founding of LWR, with Sylvester Michelfelder, LWF's first general secretary.

Checkpoint

Lutheran World Relief's mission was re-examined in the sixties. Whether by design or simply as a reaction to changing situations, new directions were being taken, new services being offered.

Until 1960 Africa had been given little attention. Only a limited amount of supplies had been sent to Tanganyika and one-time aid had been allocated to Madagascar because of a series of cyclones and floods. By 1969 five African nations were receiving assistance; in that year alone more than a million dollars worth of supplies went to that continent. More than half were given to what had become Tanzania but substantial amounts were allocated to Nigeria and Liberia, with smaller shipments to Ethiopia and Zambia.[1] Lutheran missionaries from the U.S. had been working in all of these countries over a period of many years.

LWR had supplied nothing for Latin America until 1959, when supplementary food for 29,000 people and clothing for 20,000 were contributed in support of a material aid and self-help program conducted by an agency for Protestant churches in Chile. The needs came from no particular catastrophe, but from endemic conditions, including an exceedingly high infant mortality rate. During the next decade more than three million dollars worth of supplies were provided for the work there.[2]

Since similar conditions existed in Brazil, assistance was offered there in 1960 and supplies valued at nearly 14 million dollars were provided over the next ten years. With the approval of Brazilian church officials, a pastor of the Augustana Lutheran Church, John A. Nasstrom, was sent to Brazil to help determine where the greatest needs existed, and, through consultation, to organize a program to help the destitute. A long-range purpose of the plan was to deepen concern for Christian social welfare programs among the Protestant churches of the country. In both Brazil and Chile, Lutheran World Relief was cooperating with Church World Service, the National Council of Churches' agency.

In the sixties LWR continued work begun earlier in Asian countries suffering from the effects of wars, but concern for the long-range needs of Korea, Taiwan, and Hong Kong was given new emphasis. The ongoing predicament of India commanded more and more attention until, in 1969, India was receiving more than two and one-half million dollars worth of supplies, two-thirds of the total allocation going to all of Asia.

In the Middle East Lutheran World Relief continued to assist the Palestinians, whose plight remained unchanged while they challenged Israel's existence and Israel refused to grant them political rights.

Looking to the Future

LWR's new services required different commitments from the ones prevailing in the agency's beginning. In Germany and in most of Europe the leadership and potential material resources had been so abundant that, before long, the nations could resume their self-sufficiency and share with less prosperous peoples.

Conditions elsewhere in the world were much more complex. Ove Nielsen, Bernard Confer's executive assistant, who was often delegated by Confer to prepare LWR's Annual Report, described the situation in that document for 1962: "The time has come when Lutheran World Relief, while continuing to assist hungry multitudes who rightfully look to us for gifts of food, clothing and medical supplies, should, to the extent resources can be made available, also address more of its attention to the basic factors which underlie the problems of hunger, inadequate shelter and disease. Feeding, clothing and giving medical supplies become more meaningful if at the same time people are helped to provide for their future needs. This may require embarking on new programs in some areas, or the addition of a new dimension to existing programs."

Nielsen cited, as examples of such developments, the creation of small irrigation systems, the construction of community centers and roads, the establishment of cooperatives, and education for changes in crop patterns and dietary habits. All of this was in line with evolving theories of national economic development; the task of voluntary agencies like LWR was now seen as taking the initiative to sponsor pilot projects in technical assistance and community development, counting on governments and private enterprise to carry on from there. An oriental proverb became a guiding principle: "You can give a man a fish and feed him for a day; you can teach a man to fish and feed him for a lifetime." Before long, not only men but women were given more attention in the formula and, still later, this saying was to be revised to reflect the recognition that learning to fish would have little value without having access to the pond. In the sixties, however, the prospect of learning to fish was enough to kindle the hope that millions of people could be lifted from poverty, ignorance, and disease.

One outcome of this new emphasis was the establishment of food-for-work projects, enlisting the needy in participating in development efforts while feeding their families. Lutheran World Relief helped to convince the U.S. government that this was appropriate and wise. In Korea after the war, when it was necessary to build dams and roads, LWR representatives began to use food as wages. From Washington to New York came instructions "to cease and desist because this was seen as payment for food, and food had to be distributed without cost to the recipient, and it was therefore a violation of the regulation." LWR knew that a government official on the scene in Korea, Jack Mills, had approved the idea, so he was enlisted to convince colleagues of its validity. After extensive negotiations there was a complete turnabout and within a year the government agencies wanted everyone to employ food-for-work programs as much as possible. Instead of being simply a gift from a distant benefactor, food was seen as something to be earned by labor.[3]

In the sixties U.S. officials, prodded by reports from United Nations agencies, were also becoming more aware of the likelihood of impending, widespread famine. Population was rising spectacularly in many countries, partly because the mortality rate was being improved by advances in medicine and public health measures, but domestic food production was decreasing. Authorities claimed that enough food could be produced for all people if restraints were taken off American agriculture, and if the more economically developed countries could come forward with increased material aid and technical assistance. At least some administrators and members of Congress began thinking less of reduction in surplus stocks than in planning toward permanent freedom from hunger.[4]

No Easy Answer

Even if enough food could be grown, there was no assurance that the hungry would be fed. Social and political factors in many countries resulted in drastically uneven distribution of resources. Welfare was obviously linked with justice. To go beyond temporary relief to lasting development would require more than sending food and clothing. In 1960 Stewart Herman, then staff member of the National Lutheran Council, addressed this issue on behalf of Lutheran World Relief when he spoke to a conference in Washington appraising progress made under the government's "Food for Peace" program. He contended that U.S. efforts to alleviate poor living conditions in Latin America "should be tied tightly to raising the standards of personal and public welfare." This called for a policy, he said, "that steers a careful course away from calculated charity or the protection of foreign investments."[5]

LWR, along with other voluntary agencies, was obviously rethinking the nature of its task. One result was to question an assumption of early development efforts that Western patterns of industrial and agricultural development were applicable everywhere. More attention had to be given to the cultural, climatic, and geographic conditions of each area.

Through the fifties Lutheran World Relief's primary function had been to react to needs and opportunities. Questions were raised about directions taken, but decisions had to be made quickly and results were encouraging. In the sixties the agency was entering a new era, featuring situations different from any anticipated by the founders. There was still a sense of urgency and work could not be interrupted, but staff and board members had to give time and attention to considering the principles under which new ventures would be undertaken. It was this realization that had led in 1959 to the appointment of the policy committee mentioned in chapter 5, and it was 1961 before a report was available.

Policy Statement

The committee of LWR Board members appointed in 1959, consisting of Paul Empie as chairperson, Henry Whiting, and Werner Kuntz, worked diligently on their assignment to formulate a policy statement. Other directors were invited to make suggestions and the theology of the document was reviewed. Finally, Philip A. Johnson, then executive secretary of the Department of Public Relations of the National Lutheran Council, was invited to rewrite the manuscript. It was submitted in April of 1961 and, after considerable discussion, the board authorized another revision that was adopted on May 26, 1961, after still other suggestions were incorporated.

Most of the document simply combined a review of LWR's origins with a statement of what had become operating principles. The report could estimate that, by 1961, 10 million people in more than 35 countries had received some form of help through LWR. During those 15 years the value of assistance given averaged nearly $10 million annually. A little more than half of that amount represented the value of U.S. surplus commodities; the other half, gifts of cash, clothing, and other supplies, came mostly from Lutheran congregations.

After a reminder that "conflict, calamity, and suffering are inescapable aspects of the human situation," the statement described LWR's "motivation and principles" for responding to such afflictions:

> Christian concern for the relief of suffering should not spring alone from pity for human misery. It is God's own overflowing goodness in freely granting forgiveness and eternal life through faith in Jesus Christ which is both well-spring and motivation for Christian giving. "We love, because he first loved us."

> Thus constrained, Christians seek to alleviate human need, and by so doing give tangible expression to their belief that they serve God truly by ministering to their neighbors.

Specific guidelines indicated the conditions under which Lutheran World Relief would undertake to offer assistance. For example, assurance would be required that supplies would be permitted to enter a country free of duty and were not to be bartered or sold. Where LWR did not have its own supervising staff, supplies were to be distributed by agencies functioning in harmony with LWR policies. Directions were given for preparing the description of a proposed project, including a clear financial statement and provision for review of the work.

Leading or Supporting Role?

The only parts of the statement bordering on controversy dealt with meeting long-range needs, and the different functions of government and church in undertaking this responsibility. After acknowledging that "the primary thrust of Lutheran World Relief" was to alleviate suffering in emergencies, the document recognized the prevalence of endemic need and said that the agency was "prepared to act in instances where it deems that its aid may help to improve the lot of people in such areas." This apparent promise was qualified immediately by the next sentence: "Lutheran World Relief regards large-scale relief programs of a long-term nationwide character to be typically the responsibility of governments rather than of private voluntary agencies." The statement attempted to clarify the roles of LWR and government in two significant paragraphs:

Lutheran World Relief may accept contributions of commodities for relief purposes from government, to be integrated into its own programs. Such contributions may be accepted in order to meet emergency conditions in certain areas, or for transitional situations, pending the establishment of inter-governmental programs and the development of more adequate indigenous facilities. As a general principle, Lutheran World Relief will not accept donations of commodities from governments which would, in its opinion, distort its character by overbalancing contributions from its own constituency.

The intent of Lutheran World Relief in accepting donations of commodities from governments is to cooperate in the relief of needy persons solely within the context of overlapping humanitarian concerns. Lutheran World Relief may accept cash reimbursement from governments for the cost of shipping. However, receipt of funds from governments as contributions to or reimbursement for administrative costs of the program of Lutheran World Relief would, in our estimation, vitiate the Christian and voluntary aspects of the proper character of this agency and so is unacceptable in principle.[6]

The statement encountered some criticism for apparently conceding too much to government, and underplaying the role of church agencies in going beyond relief to development. References to the distinctively Christian function of Lutheran World Relief also seemed to be somewhat vague and general. Motivation was clear, but what about expression? When working through secular agencies in lands with no presence of Christian churches, how could LWR make an authentic witness to the faith? Similar questions would surface periodically during the following years. Lutheran World Relief was heading in new directions, but was its destination where the churches wanted to go? The policy statement answered some questions but only sharpened others.

LWR staff members saw in the statement support for extending development efforts. For the annual meeting of the board in late January, 1963, they submitted a report proposing more active involvement in community development. They called attention to a deepening desire on the part of their fellow workers in other lands to provide services of more long-term benefit. Those partners were saying that it was important to help those who were suffering, but were asking, "Is it not more important to prevent suffering?" [7] Bernard Confer was advocating employment by LWR of technical personnel to serve in communities where people had demonstrated willingness to help themselves. Ove Nielsen maintained that funds should be allocated for longer-range efforts even if this meant, owing to limited resources, smaller programs of food distribution.[8]

Reconsidered Resignation

Franklin Fry, as founding president of Lutheran World Relief, stayed in close touch with all that was happening in the agency, and he was troubled by what he feared might become a precarious deviation from its original purposes. He was afraid that LWR would be drawn away from its distinctively Christian character by the nature of the new tasks. He acknowledged the necessity of community development but was reluctant to see Lutheran World Relief becoming heavily engaged in it. He was afraid that a disproportionate share of resources would be required, for example, to train leaders abroad. He wondered whether LWR's insistence on working only with the most needy might be a handicap in identifying potential leaders; he suspected that the search might have to go beyond this segment of the population.

Fry was reluctant to see LWR become more involved in relationships with governments, believing that the U.S. government should take full responsibility for disposition of surplus commodities by negotiating directly with the governments of receiving countries. He was aware of problems in places like Taiwan, where voluntary agencies could not be sure that all recipients of aid were actually the most needy. Once, in fact, the government there had urged that supplies be made available to members of Chiang Kai Shek's army, who were not among the poorest of the poor.[9]

For various reasons, then, Fry told Confer that he intended to resign from the presidency and from the board at the first meeting of LWR in 1963, when directors and officers were to be elected for new terms. Days before that meeting Confer took Paul Empie and Ove Nielsen with him to meet with Fry for a thorough discussion of the issues. When Fry remained firm in his intention, a farewell luncheon was planned to honor him during what was to be his final meeting.

What happened between then and noon of January 29, 1963, is somewhat muddled by differing recollections, but other friends of Fry, including Henry Whiting, did urge Fry to remain in office. At a National Lutheran Council meeting just prior to the LWR sessions, the development issue was aired and it became obvious that there was strong support for the direction proposed by staff. Nevertheless, when the LWR meetings began, Fry still indicated his intention to resign. Directors suggested that the new approach to development could be supported if there could be agreement on certain emphases and limitations. LWR could counsel with churches abroad and help them in their development efforts. The board decided to conduct a new study to look into these possibilities.

By noon Fry had decided to remain in office and accepted re-election to both board membership and presidency. Now it was time for the luncheon, for which Paul Empie and Edwin Nerger had been appointed to make farewell speeches of tribute. Nerger decided to leave his in the form originally intended, prompting laughter to which Fry responded with his usual vigor. Empie expressed joy that Fry was remaining in office, but took the occasion to say that Lutheran World Relief was now strong enough to continue its work no matter who was in charge. Fry commented, "Yes, Paul, that's true." Confer later said, "Fry was never more supportive to me than after that meeting." [10] The concerns that bothered Fry at this time deserved consideration and received it from LWR staff and board partly because of his forceful expression of them.

A Critical Review

To conduct the new study that had been authorized, a new committee was needed, so Henry Whiting was appointed as chairperson, with Werner Kuntz and Kenneth Priebe, an American Lutheran Church stewardship executive elected to the board in 1959, as the other members. They were ready in two months with their report. Almost twice as long as the policy statement adopted two years earlier, it was titled, "A Critical Review" because it devoted considerable space to an appraisal of Lutheran World Relief's operations. No significant changes in the policy statement were recommended but the new document did focus attention more clearly on helping people to help themselves.

One observation, among others, related relief to development: "The experience of past years has indicated that assisting in meeting genuine physical need can be a stimulant to a developing sense of social responsibility to the community at large. When congregations or committees give serious attention to ameliatory relief, it is not long until they discuss other ways in which the churches may relate themselves constructively to the society in which they function."

Community development was endorsed. "Projects in the field of social and economic development can be instrumental in promoting individual responsibility, in fostering an appreciation for voluntary action. They can be of aid to people in becoming self-sustaining economically. In addition, projects may be sufficiently successful to serve as beacons to neighboring communities." Examples cited were agricultural and marketing cooperatives, road building, credit unions, and parent education programs.

Questions concerning Christian witness were also treated in the document. Where supplies were being distributed through secular agencies there could be little recognition of the givers' motivation. The use of government surplus commodities required identifying their source, making identification with churches even more dubious. In many situations, however, there were individuals whose dedication was an impressive testimony to the faith.

When the board considered the committee's document, special attention was given to this issue, and supplementary statements were added. One dealt specifically with witness: "Without detracting from its policy of providing assistance on the basis of greatest need without discrimination as to creed, race, or political affiliation, Lutheran World Relief recognizes that the purpose of its existence is to provide explicit Christian witness through service related to specific needs and that normally the witness will be expressed in the lives of the people who carry out the program."

To facilitate this happening, priorities for the selection of projects included two specific provisions. Special consideration was to be given to projects in regions where there was a strong Lutheran presence, and LWR was to consider service projects that would "provide for assistance in the extension and strengthening of the life and witness of the church." [11]

Future boards and staffs would continue to wrestle with the relationship in witness between word and deed. There was no question as to the essential nature of both; how best to contribute to the abundance or fullness of life promised by Christ remained an objective worth ongoing exploration. Paul Empie summarized LWR's position in the sixties when he wrote, "Providing material relief in itself is not a sign of Christian love—atheists and agnostics often do the same thing with equal compassion and dedication. Yet if there is no tangible demonstration that the church really cares about human needs, the obvious conclusion is that her talk about love is phony." He maintained that relief "should not be an instrument of evangelism," but that "the style of service and Christian personalities of staff bear witness to Christ." [12]

Financial Concerns

LWR board and staff members struggled during the sixties with other matters of a very practical nature. One of them was the concern for continuing financial support. Would Lutherans continue to contribute to programs less sensational than postwar devastation? Some of the new projects would require large sums that would be more difficult to raise because they would not command the public media coverage that accompanied catastrophes. Whereas most of the cost of relief efforts was being covered from government funds, most of the support for development projects would have to be supplied by LWR constituents.

Questions about continuing finances had been the subject of conversations since the early fifties but were now complicated by synodical realignments among churches of the National Lutheran Council. The eight churches in the Council were realigned into what became two new bodies, The American Lutheran Church, formed in 1960, and the Lutheran Church in America, formed in 1962.

In the new churches Lutheran World Action, the primary source for their support of LWR, was made a regular budget item rather than a separate appeal. Church officials had been considering this possibility for several years. Some maintained that separate appeals allowed enthusiasts for special causes to drain money from the more essential functions of the churches, as determined by the best informed executives. Paul Empie opposed putting LWA on the budgets, claiming that pastors often told him that such appeals were "the easiest money we ever raised," and that the contributions did not come at the expense of other giving, but that the other giving increased simultaneously. The new churches, however, were facing their own financial problems and the decision held; funding for relief and development was included in the regular budget.

This was a potentially serious blow to LWR, because Lutheran World Action, with Rollin Shaffer taking the lead in generating publicity, had provided most of the promotional and educational materials for national distribution. In 25 years 25 motion pictures and 34 filmstrips had been produced. With no special access to congregational channels, news about global needs would receive much less attention than before. Lutheran World Action was not officially discontinued until 1977 but its activities were severely restricted. Printed matter, for example, was limited to the contents of an ordinary business-sized envelope mailed once a year.[13]

Tight budgets, especially in difficult economic times, would never provide for creative efforts in dealing with world conditions, and some leaders favored a combination of budgetary funding for basic operations and special appeals for projects. Even before the end of the decade a special appeal was approved because of the Biafra crisis, and in the seventies the whole matter was reconsidered. Until then, income from the churches did not decline sharply but neither did it increase enough to allow for the degree of expansion desired by staff.

During the sixties also, the two new churches, ALC and LCA, and The Lutheran Church—Missouri Synod began exploring expanded efforts in cooperation. In 1967 they established the Lutheran Council in the United States of America (LCUSA), to act together in many of the tasks formerly undertaken by the National Lutheran Council. Since LCMS was not a member of the Lutheran World Federation, representatives of the other churches continued to act as the United States National Committee of the Lutheran World Federation. They adopted the title, Lutheran World Ministries, for this function and elected Paul Empie as executive director. The name of Lutheran World Action was retained to channel funds to both the LWF and Lutheran World Relief.

Neither the formation of LCUSA nor its later demise had a significant impact on Lutheran World Relief. Differences in theological positions between The Lutheran Church—Missouri Synod and the other church bodies never threatened LWR actions. There could be no doctrinal disagreement over clear scriptural admonitions to serve the needs of the poor. Deliberations over policies were not divided along synodical lines. Even when, later in the decade, the Association of Evangelical Lutheran Churches was established by congregations separating from the LCMS, the main effect on LWR was the election of an additional director, Harold L. Hecht, to represent the AELC, which had immediately become a supporting body of LWR. The

LCMS Board of World Relief continued to engage in its own activities, including domestic aid, but also participated fully in LWR. LCMS members developed a dual loyalty, most probably not distinguishing sharply between the two similarly named agencies. Along with women from the other churches, LCMS women established personal ties with Lutheran World Relief through the investment of their handiwork.

Members of The Lutheran Church—Missouri Synod shared the uncertainty over provision for continuing support of global service. Devastating effects of the Nigeria-Biafra civil war in the late sixties brought the problem into sharp focus. The depths of LCMS concern were expressed in a resolution, "To Intensify Efforts to Alleviate World Hunger," adopted by the Synod in its July, 1969, convention. After reviewing the global prospect for mass starvation and the responsibility of Christians to meet their Lord's directive to feed the hungry, the resolution instructed the LCMS Board of Directors to realign its budget priorities, cover the basic administrative costs of the Board of World Relief, and divert $100,000 to that board. Congregations and members were challenged to "change the past and present practice of 'token giving' to 'sacrificial giving' for this critical need." Members were also exhorted to "urge our governmental officials to reassess our national values and priorities in order to deal more effectively with this serious and heartless problem of world hunger." [14]

After Twenty Years, a Budget

At the end of 1964 Lutheran World Relief adopted a budget for 1965, "subject to review at each meeting." Franklin Fry and Henry Whiting had been advocating this for some time. Preparing it was one of the tasks assigned to James F. Patterson when he was appointed as an assistant executive secretary in late 1963.

The absence of a formal, operating budget did not reflect fiscal irresponsibility. LWR always submitted detailed, accurate reports of all transactions to the churches and the government. Bernard Confer, however, preferred to work without a specific financial projection to allow him greater administrative flexibility. He could claim, truthfully, that in each year there would be unexpected needs and unpredictable amounts of income. The relationship with World Service of the Lutheran World Federation was another complicating element. There was an understanding that expenses incurred in administering LWF World Service programs would be supplied by donor agencies, either directly from churches or through LWR. In 1965, for example, LWR was not called upon to supply these funds for Jordan, Hong Kong, or Tanzania, but they were needed for India.[15]

After twenty years, however, it was possible to estimate roughly the annual incidence of catastrophes and the U.S. Lutherans' share for relief. Revisions could always be made in the budget if this became necessary. Confer agreed, and contributing church bodies appreciated the move because their executives were expected to make careful projections for all budget items. Much later, it became possible to establish a reserve fund to prepare for emergencies.

Despite budgetary constraints, Lutheran World Relief did not weaken its stand against possible misuse of government funds. Under consideration again was a proposal to amend Public Law 480 to allow voluntary agencies to use counterpart funds, the foreign currencies accrued to the U.S. Government from the distribution of surplus commodities abroad, to finance the cost of administering their projects. Catholic Relief Services and CARE favored the change but LWR opposed it. Paul Empie and Bernard Confer testified before congressional committees, giving three reasons why LWR continued to favor the system by which voluntary agencies bore the costs of distributing commodities:

1. It avoids the temptation for agencies to mushroom their programs out of proportion to their own resources and beyond the point of manageability.
2. It protects the voluntary character of the religious agencies by requiring them to finance a substantial part of their program.
3. It underscores the necessity that religious agencies should not become, either in fact or in the estimate of the public, instruments of government and channels for achieving the purposes of U.S. foreign policy.[16]

Beyond Relief

The extensive deliberations over policy matters never interfered with the ongoing work of Lutheran World Relief. In the newer focus on Asia, Africa, and Latin America, there was still need for food and clothing. Shipments of clothing and related items averaged 5 million pounds annually in the sixties. Availability of government surplus food was reduced during the decade, but more than 40 million pounds were still being shipped in 1969.

Needs sometimes occurred in unexpected places. In 1961 a famine developed among Masai tribes in Tanganyika, now Tanzania. The Masai were regarded as among the least likely candidates for aid from the United States. They herded their cattle, sheep, and goats over thousands of square miles of northern Tanganyika and parts of Kenya, and generally survived the most difficult conditions. It was said of them that they would sell everything they could possibly sell before accepting help from the outside. When, however, their area was engulfed in a state of "convulsion" as a result of both too little and too much water—devastating drought in some sections and inundating floods in others—they were grateful for aid. Lutheran World Relief stepped in with shipments of 100,000 pounds of powdered milk and 500,000 pounds of cornmeal.[1]

Both food and clothing were still badly needed in Hong Kong. The Lutheran World Federation was at work there, and support was coming from many countries, but most of its food, clothing, and medicines came from Lutheran World Relief. The demand for blankets was so great that, in 1961, arrangements were made to have quilts manufactured there from cotton supplied by the U.S. Government. For this purpose 256 bales were shipped. At that time there were still an estimated 50,000 refugees sleeping on Hong Kong streets[2].

Needs for clothing also continued elsewhere but became more specialized. Western styles were less acceptable in Asia and Africa but there was still a demand for work clothes for men, children's garments, and blankets or quilts. Spring and fall appeals in thousands of congregations were planned and promoted by some 75 key leaders from inter-synodical committees, welfare societies, pastors' conferences, women's organizations, synods, and districts. In a number of instances commercial trucking companies transported the collections long distances to warehouses without cost to donors or to Lutheran World Relief, a practice that continues in some areas to this day.

Requests for large numbers of Kiddies Kits continued to come from various countries, including Ethiopia. A new Project Esther called for the purchase of denim cloth to be patterned and sewn into dresses for girls and shorts for boys, all between seven and eleven years of age. Bright colors were recommended and the denim was specified because of its durability where washing was done by scrubbing on rocks.

Lutheran World Relief also collected tons of soap to be sent overseas. When someone speculated that there were probably thousands of motels where soap, barely used, was thrown out daily, a letter was sent to congregations asking members to explore this possibility. The appeal started a chain reaction in Milwaukee. The first motel operators to be solicited were so enthusiastic that they related the word to the Greater Milwaukee Hotel-Motel Association, and there were immediate indications that up to 2,500 bars of soap could be contributed daily to the drive. Response was great enough to provide substantial shipments to a number of countries and the program became ongoing. Small pieces were melted into larger bars for convenience in shipping and distributing.[3]

One 80-year-old woman, Mrs. Erma Wilson of Columbiana, Ohio, contributed to the soap collection in her own, ingenious way. Working in the former coal cellar of her home, she manufactured soap from grease and fat obtained from a local pizza parlor and friends. Buckets of bacon fat and lard were left by neighbors on her doorstep. Using large kettles, she rendered the soap through the laborious process of cleaning, mixing with lye, cutting and drying. She thought the 33 pounds produced in her first year was "a goodly amount" but after awhile she was able to increase her output until she could ship more than 1,000 pounds in a year.[4]

New Emphasis

Much of Lutheran World Relief's work in the sixties reflected the newer emphasis going beyond temporary aid. Even where catastrophes were addressed, attention was given to the conditions that would prevail after the crisis had ended. With each intervention, consideration was given to needs other than food and clothing.

LWR efforts in Korea were a good example of the new direction being taken. Several years after fighting had ended, large shipments of food, clothing, and medicine were still being sent but development programs were also being undertaken and much of the food was being applied to work required for those projects. As elsewhere, LWR channeled its services through a domestic organization, in this case Korean Church World Service (KCWS). Both LWR and Church World Service supported KCWS. Following James Claypool and Carl Hult as LWR representative, Abner Batalden became deputy director of KCWS in 1963.

The most ambitious project of KCWS in the sixties was the reclamation of more than 2,000 acres of land from the ocean at Dae Duk. Seventeen hundred workers, both men and women representing 700 families of refugees from North Korea, labored for more than three years, carrying many tons of dirt, clay, gravel, and stones on A-frames fastened to their backs and shoulders. They built huge dams, up to a mile in length, approximately 150 feet wide at the base, 25 to 50 feet high, and 25 feet wide at the crest. Then they leveled the reclaimed area and cleared off the stones. Batalden's Korean counterpart in the program department of CWS did much of the negotiating with national and provincial officials, the workers' committee, and the supervising engineer. Together, the two had to work in harmony with U.S. agencies and with New York offices of LWR and CWS to keep the donated food, clothing, medicine, and other supplies flowing as needed.

The project created both a reservoir, actually a lake covering 160 acres fed by mountain waters, and a huge plain ready for cultivation. When the work was completed the government met its promise to grant land with legal title from the newly cleared area to each of the families who had provided laborers. Each plot consisted of a hectare (2.47 acres), close to the average holding of Korean farmers, and meant that each worker-family would now have a farm home.

More than ten years after the project was completed, Batalden returned to Dae Duk to see what difference had been made in the lives of the people. He looked out upon "a mammoth sea of gold," barley being harvested and piled into large mounds, ready to be bagged. Nearby were also small plots of thickly planted rice shoots, awaiting the completion of the barley harvest. At that time the ground would be plowed again, flooded from the reservoir, and rice would be planted as the second crop of the year. Farmers were also raising vegetables and catching fish stocked in the lake.

Batalden learned from area officials that cereal grains worth more than $3 million were being produced each year on the Dae Duk project land, while the value of all supplies contributed to the project, most of it from the U.S. government, had been estimated at $700,000. Impressive as this sounds to market-oriented investors, the human outcomes were even more significant. Thirty-five hundred people from 700 families had been transformed from unemployed, homeless refugees to self-supporting residents of thatch-roofed houses. Their diligence in the project had set a good pattern for their continued employment. With some additional assistance their small villages soon included an elementary school, a clinic, and small business operations necessary for daily life. The accomplishments so impressed the government that similar ventures were allowed and even supported elsewhere.[5]

Experiences like the one at Dae Duk encouraged Lutheran World Relief in diversifying its services. The sixties were even described in some circles as the "decade of development." LWR facilitated construction of large irrigation wells, scores of water retention dams, hundreds of miles of farm-to-market roads, and many hundreds of schools and community centers. It sponsored teams for family planning, projects in nutrition, and health care through service centers.

Not all projects involved major expenditures. In the Cooch Behar district of West Bengal, India, a Lutheran missionary had assisted in resettling refugee families in a number of small communities. Some land was granted by the government and additional acreage was purchased by funds from Sweden and from the Bengal Refugee Service, with which the Lutheran World Federation had a direct relationship. Gifts from various sources had made possible the building of homes and a school, and the digging of fresh water wells. To make the communities operative and sustainable, a number of important needs remained unfunded and Lutheran World Relief responded to an appeal for help. First, a road was elevated to serve as a dike to protect the homes and fruit trees of the forty refugee families in one of the communities. Two water pumps were installed for irrigation to prepare for the time when rainfall would be short. Most of this was accomplished on a food-for-work basis, requiring 60 days if both husbands and wives participated. Only $1,904 in cash was needed, plus 15,680 pounds of wheat provided by the U.S. government. Next, the road was extended around two of the colonies to furnish a means for transport of farm products to market. This was also accomplished primarily on a food-for-work basis, requiring 3,500 man/woman-days and 17,425 pounds of wheat. The only financial expenditures for LWR were the costs of material for two bridges and wages for major earth moving and supervision, totaling $1,566. Next, LWR undertook to support the construction of a reservoir needed for irrigation, water storage, and fish raising. Another irrigation pump was also needed. For this project 8,000 pounds of wheat and $1,040 were provided. One additional project required only $404 for purchase of bamboo and other materials to construct a latrine shelter, necessary for minimal protection against hook worms.[6]

Other LWR programs in the sixties were oriented more directly to persons than to construction. Funds were granted Korean Church World Service for the employment of a number of social workers. Two universities in Korea, one of which was church-related, offered undergraduate training in social welfare and KCWS provided special orientation for persons to be hired. Each social worker supported by LWR was assigned to a number of institutions, particularly those housing thousands of children made homeless by many years of war and turmoil. Heavily burdened welfare institutions were assisted in better equipping both children and adults to become more responsible citizens. Case workers also counseled with families and encouraged community development efforts. As many as ten Korean workers were employed on a temporary basis and two Americans assisted in recruiting, training, and supervision.[7]

The high birth rate in most of the poorer countries made it difficult for agricultural efforts to keep pace with increases in population. The government in India was officially committed to a program of birth control but progress was slow during the sixties. There was general agreement that major resistance came from parents who regarded large numbers of children as a form of insurance: many would die before maturity and survivors would be needed for support in old age. Other, more questionable factors affected the cultural situation. In India's Madras State, where 80% of the villagers had electricity in 1966, the birth rate was only half as large as in the nation as a whole.[8] An advance in economic well-being appeared to reduce family size.

International and voluntary agencies launched an effort to assist nations in controlling population expansion, and Lutheran World Relief made funds available for family planning projects in India, Korea, and Taiwan. When reporting on these efforts Bernard Confer called attention to documents dealing with responsible parenthood from official boards of Lutheran churches. One had been adopted by the Lutheran Church in America at its 1964 convention, another was a paper authorized by The American Lutheran Church's Commission on Research and Social Action, and the third was a pamphlet, "God's Plan for Parenthood," distributed by Concordia Publishing House of The Lutheran Church—Missouri Synod. Confer noted that they stated clearly "that God calls on men and women to be responsible parents, and they stress the value of family planning and conception control in promoting the well-being of the family." [9]

In Chile, when local churches and voluntary agencies studied relief programs, they agreed that greater attention had to be focused on basic causes. They decided to give more attention to adult education and community development programs, including studies of leadership training, agricultural extension, home economics, health, and literacy. All reflected a philosophy that "education must precede or at least run parallel with action programs." LWR joined in the start of the effort in 1964 by contributing $18,000.[10]

Haven't We Been Here Before?

Halfway through the sixties, Lutheran World Relief faced a situation similar to the one that brought about its creation twenty years earlier. A dreadful war was bringing havoc to the people of a distant land. This time the war had been going on for many years and would not end for many more. Unlike in 1945, few of the victims were Lutheran, except for those fighting and dying in the U.S. military intervention. But the human tragedy was reminiscent of the devastation resulting from World War II. As before, American relief agencies had special access to the territory occupied by U.S. forces, South Vietnam.

Once again a survey team was sent to inspect conditions and to return with recommendations to guide relief operations. In 1965 at the invitation of President Johnson, Bernard Confer went on behalf of Lutheran World Relief, along with representatives of five other voluntary agencies and two government officials. The Mennonite Central Committee and Catholic Relief Services were also at work there.

The observers concluded that the most pressing problem would come from the mounting number of refugees pouring into areas along the coast or up in the highlands. A million of them were expected to move in by the end of the year. Rural areas were constantly subject to guerilla action by Vietcong and transportation was hazardous. The South Vietnam government was undertaking relief programs to provide minimal rations and some communities were trying to arrange for housing and medical services. LWR joined with the Mennonite Central Committee and Church World Service to form the agency known as Vietnam Christian Service. Since the Mennonites had been on the scene for more than a decade, they began administering the program.

Aid to Vietnam recapitulated, between 1965 and 1970, LWR's 25 years of experience. Emphasis moved from relief to personal rehabilitation to community development. Vietnamese gradually replaced expatriates in supervisory positions. In one important respect, however, the Vietnam venture was confronted by distinctive hazards.

Tensions at Home and Abroad

Because of the division among Americans concerning U.S. involvement in the war, some people believed that American agencies should stay out of Vietnam. Any attempt to serve there would be "taking sides" in the conflict. LWR would be identified as a tool of both the U.S. and South Vietnam governments, from whom permission would have to be secured just to enter the country. There would be little opportunity to push for social change or even peace; services to the south would disregard suffering across the shifting border. Any claims that some aid would reach victims from the north only aroused opposition from Americans who regarded such action as disloyal.

Bernard Confer had an answer to the objection that offering social services which should be provided locally would save that government money to be spent on weapons. He saw the role of LWR principally as one of supplemental service, "particularly to those pockets of people who are missed by governmental programs which, by necessity, have a mass approach." He admitted that limitations existed in Vietnam work but saw these as practical problems rather than political restraints. On his recommendation Lutheran World Relief never became involved in shipping volumes of supplies to South Vietnam as large as were sent to Europe or even India, Korea, Hong Kong, Jordan, Taiwan, or Brazil. Instead, attention was focused as soon as possible on preparations for the future.[11]

In Vietnam the cooperative effort was not without internal tensions. There were bound to be disagreements among persons from different denominations, different educational and social backgrounds, relating to predominantly Buddhist communities. The massive effort was undertaken so hastily that there was a lack of integrated philosophy and programs. The prospect of risking government displeasure by visiting political prisoners raised questions. Despite these prevailing conditions, Vietnam Christian Service made significant contributions to the survival and prospects for rehabilitation in Vietnam. Overriding all tensions and uncertainties, the ecumenical agency operated on the basis of fundamental goals, two of which were "to carry out a personalized, efficient and impartial ministry to persons in need," and "to witness to the cross of Christ and to the reconciling power of love in the midst of violence, fear, hate and despair." [12]

To pursue that goal in the situation in Vietnam at that time required an enlistment of personnel including doctors, nurses, social workers, home economists, agriculturalists, community development educators, and material aid specialists. Of the $100,000 appropriated for LWR's entrance into South Vietnam, half was earmarked for personnel and the rest divided between program and the purchase of supplies.

The Hope Corps

The need for persons with so many different qualifications to serve abroad on behalf of Lutheran World Relief led to the recruitment of many new ambassadors of faith. They were often employed for longer periods of time than the representatives who went to Europe after World War II. After establishing good working relationships with local agencies in one country, they were often assigned to another. Like the founders of the U.S. Peace Corps, they were stirred by a vision that went beyond immediate tasks. The hope they brought with them was as important as the material aid, and was to be shared. Often their hopes were bolstered by what they discovered in the lives of the people with whom they worked; there was a contagion of hope growing out of the partnership of working together.

Two young Lutheran couples, Neil and Marta Brenden and Jerry and Judy Aaker, joined the staff in Vietnam early in July, 1965. All had completed language studies, three of them were graduate social workers, and Judy Aaker was a nurse. All would serve LWR in different capacities for many years. Larry Roth and Joseph Sprunger were also enlisted later for leadership in New York after ministering in Vietnam. At one time or another during the decade of operation by Vietnam Christian Service, 23 staff members were employees of LWR. The only casualty among them was Gloria Anne Redlin, a nurse from Oshkosh, Wisconsin, who was serving in a hospital for mountain people. She was killed by gunfire in 1970.[13]

Abner Batalden and his wife, Martha, began serving in Korea but went from there to Vietnam, India, and Bangladesh. Harald Hans Lund, after eight years in Yugoslavia, was sent to Nigeria in 1969 as a trouble shooter to deal with the crisis there. Edwin Medley, who had been a city manager in California, applied his organizational skills to the situation in Taiwan, then went to Bangladesh and Jordan. Dozens of others were recruited for similar assignments in the sixties and later. The need for their skills became more immediate when, in 1965, the United States Agency for International Development (U.S. AID) established a Special Self-Help and Development Activities Fund, supporting a range of projects with subsidy limited to $10,000. This approach had the advantage of backing programs that were limited in scope and could be monitored for effectiveness, but it did require more time and personnel for administration.

Lutheran World Relief has always insisted that its participation in projects is to be non-operational. LWR staff members do not actually carry out the work of the project; they cooperate with local agencies and individuals to see that the tasks are accomplished. This is important for the sake of sustaining what is being begun. Residents must be prepared to take initiative and responsibility when LWR is no longer present. Sometimes, of course, the line between operational and non-operational is a thin one; when a well is to be drilled and the LWR representative is the one who knows how it must be done, the line must be crossed, but only temporarily.

Before a project is to be undertaken in a country, a representative from LWR will have explored the situation there, evaluating elements of the political situation that could affect the project and determining which existing agency is capable of undertaking the operation. Preferably, the partner will be church-related, provided LWR is assured that its policy of serving the needy without discrimination will be observed. Possible tensions among the churches must also be considered. In Chile in 1966, for example, the Pentecostal churches had "frozen out" the other Protestant churches, causing them to sever ties with the recognized ecumenical social service agency.[14]

When conditions do not constitute an obvious emergency, the LWR representative must engage in thorough consultation concerning any proposal to be submitted to the central office. Information is shared concerning successes and failures from similar efforts in other lands. LWR staff members must balance their sympathetic involvement in the community with their knowledge of Lutheran World Relief's resources and limitations.

Additions to overseas staff would eventually require significant expansion in the New York office. During the sixties, however, a few executives, aided by loyal support people, continued to carry the load. Candace Sadler had become administrative assistant in 1959 and continued in that position until 1971. Bernard Confer traveled regularly to lands where LWR was involved, and carefully analyzed recommendations from deployed staff to be certain that they were in line with established policy. More frequent contact between New York and overseas was the primary responsibility of Ove Nielsen. For years Nielsen related to project directors throughout Africa, Asia, and the Middle East. When James Patterson came to the staff in 1963 he was assigned to coordinate programs in Latin America and the Middle East. Later there would be further division of these responsibilities.

Carl Lorey died in 1961 after thirteen years of devoted service. His supervision of the extensive warehousing and shipping activities had been characterized by thoroughness and efficiency. His replacement, Arthur Johnsen, stayed for more than six years until resigning to return to the commercial field. He was succeeded by Kenneth F. Killen, who had assisted both Lorey and Johnsen, chiefly in the area of claims either for ocean freight reimbursement or for insured damage or loss of relief cargo. He had come to LWR in 1957. When being interviewed prior to that appointment, Killen had been told by Confer that the position was temporary, with no provision for unemployment compensation. Killen was still with Lutheran World Relief in 1995 as director for material resources. When Confer retired at the end of 1981 Killen jokingly asked him whether he, Killen, could now regard his position as permanent.[15]

Change at the Helm

Franklin Clark Fry died on June 6, 1968, after giving leadership to Lutheran World Relief for nearly 23 years. He began as the newly elected president of one Lutheran body, but became increasingly influential nationally, ecumenically, and globally. In his extensive travels he was always alert to explore opportunities and responsibilities for Lutheran World Relief. In his communications with pastors he reminded them regularly of the mission of service to the world's needy people.

Bernard Confer maintained that Fry's leadership in the National Council of Churches was instrumental in relating Lutheran World Relief appropriately to the mainstream of American Protestantism, and that his positions with the World Council of Churches and the Lutheran World Federation were vital to LWR's outreach abroad.[16]

Fry was noted for his sharp mind and his incisiveness in presiding over a meeting. This made it all the more remarkable that he also attempted to make certain that all participants in deliberations had the opportunity to express viewpoints and convictions. He could be dominating and even caustic, but he could also reveal a sense of his own humanity. Once when Ove Nielsen had been courageous enough to express, in private, that he did not think that Fry had "done right" by a person being dismissed from the staff of Church World Service, Fry responded, "Ove, you're supposed to have faith in God, not me."[17]

At their meeting following Fry's death, members of the LWR Board of Directors adopted the following memorial citation summarizing Fry's contribution to Lutheran World Relief, a statement that actually summarizes most of Lutheran World Relief's accomplishments in its first quarter-century:

> The Board of Directors of Lutheran World Relief thanks God for the marvelously fruitful life of Dr. Franklin Clark Fry. The array of his exceptional gifts, supported by boundless energy, not only made a lasting impact on all of Christendom but also enabled him to play a leading role in the alleviation of physical misery and suffering.

> As a founder and incorporator and as presiding officer of Lutheran World Relief since its beginning, Dr. Fry exemplified the prompt and compassionate response of the Lutherans of America to the needy of the world.

> His colleagues on the Board of Directors express their heartfelt gratitude for his creative leadership and wise guidance in the enterprise which has had such a significant part in the unprecedented achievements of religious groups in saving uncounted lives and ministering to the needs of millions of helpless victims of war and disaster in our time.

> Dr. Fry not only represented Lutheran World Relief before the highest circles of government both in this country and overseas, but also played an influential and possibly a decisive role in the policy determination by which the United States allowed American relief agencies to come so quickly to the assistance of defeated and prostrate Germany following World War II.

While the bitter Korean conflict was still in progress, Dr. Fry helped to found American Relief for Korea to facilitate assistance for that stricken land.

Dr. Fry was of service to the entire circle of voluntary agencies by sharing his insights regarding the appropriate roles of denominational, interdenominational, and secular agencies, as well as the proper relationships between private and governmental agencies. More than once he was a courageous spokesman for positions which were unpopular but right.

In the name and the spirit of our Savior-Lord the directors of Lutheran World Relief have been privileged to serve with Dr. Fry, and record thanks for this servant of God who has helped to bless the lives of nameless millions.[18]

Paul Empie was elected as only the second president of Lutheran World Relief and Robert J. Marshall, who succeeded Fry as president of the Lutheran Church in America, also replaced him on the LWR Board. Because of Lutheran World Relief's corporate nature, that board could be almost self-perpetuating; in practice officials of member churches did have a voice in recommending directors to be elected. In 1960 its membership of eight still included three of the five founders: Fry, Empie, and Markel. Empie and Markel, both from the Lutheran Church in America, were still in office at the end of the decade. Edwin Nerger and Werner Kuntz, the original Lutheran Church—Missouri Synod representatives from the early fifties, remained as members through the sixties. Adding to the LCMS representation, William F. Bruenning was elected in 1964 and, when he died in 1966, William F. Kohn replaced him. Representation from The American Lutheran Church traditionally included a national staff member and at least one parish pastor. Kenneth Priebe, a stewardship executive, served during the sixties, as did Elmer Hjortland. Henry Whiting was the third ALC member until he was replaced by John Stensvaag in 1966. At this time individual directors still nominally held the positions of secretary and treasurer of LWR, and reviewed the relevant documents, but the actual tasks of recording and reporting were staff functions.

The Next Quarter Century?

In 1970 Lutheran World Relief observed its 25th anniversary. Paul Empie recalled participating in the organizational meeting, when none of the five persons present anticipated a quarter century of continued activity. "Why was LWR continued?" he asked in an anniversary report. His answer: "Because wars are not the only evils which blight lives, and the Jericho Road goes around the world. A contemporary hymn claims, 'They will know we are Christians by our love.' How shall that love be communicated to two-thirds of the earth's population which suffers continually from disease, malnutrition, exploitation, and lack of opportunity? 'Man shall not live by bread alone' but he cannot live *without* bread!"

The same report listed a number of salient facts pointing to conditions needing to be addressed in the years ahead. They included:

- People are multiplying faster than jobs.
- The distribution of the world's people and of the world's food and goods is cruelly out of balance.
- Even though agricultural production is increasing dramatically, one-third to one-half of the world's people suffer from hunger or malnutrition.
- Infant mortality is four times as high in poor countries as in rich.
- The gap between the haves and the have-nots is getting wider.
- While nations are pouring more than 200 billion dollars a year into military arms, the rich industrial countries are not even meeting the goal of 7 billion dollars annually in development funds for the poor countries.
- Poverty is not inevitable, but it is intolerable.

Toward the end of the sixties American interest in combating global poverty seemed to be waning. Although figures for the gross national product and per capita income reached new heights, economic aid for other countries was greatly reduced. Congressional appropriations for that purpose were the lowest since the Marshall Plan was introduced in the forties. A mere one and one-quarter percent of the federal budget was designated for foreign economic aid in 1968 in contrast to seven percent in 1951. William S. Gaud, director of the U.S. Agency for International Development, undoubtedly spoke out of considerable frustration with Congress—and citizens who voted for anybody who promised to reduce foreign aid—when he said, "Today it is not the backward Indian peasant who blocks the road to food self-sufficiency—it is the indifferent American. We have learned a lot about how to help underdeveloped countries move off dead center. We have learned less about how to help Americans visualize the grim future that faces them and their children so long as more than half of the world ends each day hungry and homeless."[19]

It was easy to be discouraged about prospects for improvement in the global situation as the sixties came to an end. But Lutheran World Relief workers and supporters did not allow such reasons to prevent them from acting courageously. Entering a new quarter century, Lutheran World Relief staff members had renewed confidence in their ability to facilitate change. They had a vision of new directions to be followed. From steps already taken, they had learned some principles to be followed and they were ready with plans to share resources and hope.

BEYOND RELIEF, the 1960s see LWR turning to "factors which underlie hunger" (p. 58). Here, a village enterprise in India.

PUBLICITY comes with partnership on a special occasion in India. LWR works overseas through local agencies.

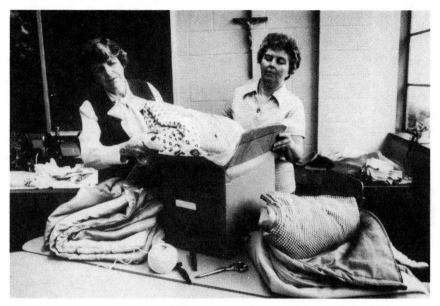

QUILTS, patchworks of cloth and love, leave parishes across the U.S. year round, ready for the next emergency.

WAREHOUSES in Maryland and Minnesota ship relief goods overseas. Other warehouses were used at different times (p.137).

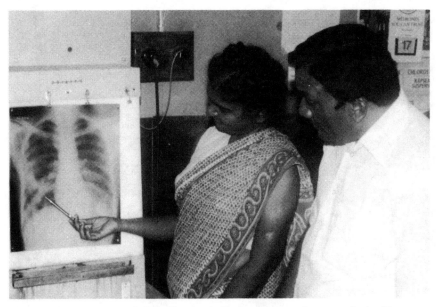

THE DRS. AROLE, Mabelle and Rajanikant, devote their lives to promoting health among the poor and weak of India (pp. 98, 150).

PRESIDENTS David Preus, J. A. O. Preus, and Robert Marshall (left to right) represent three 1970s Lutheran churches with common ground in LWR.

BERNIE CONFER, LWR's first full-time executive director, visits Bangladesh after a cyclone. He joined the agency in 1946 and shaped its first 35 years.

A SELF-HELP AGENCY offers workers a fair wage and a hand in management in Andra Pradesh state, India, in the 1970s.

WITH the People

Venturing beyond relief, LWR adopted a functional pattern described in different ways. Negatively, as previously observed, it was non-operational, meaning that Lutheran World Relief representatives would not carry out the actual work of a project, but would depend for its implementation on other agencies and individuals. Positively, LWR's role was to be one of accompaniment, participating in the process without dominating it. The needy were not to be regarded simply as recipients or victims; their patience and determination in the midst of desperate situations often revealed a degree of hope that was a model for more affluent partners.

Revising Abraham Lincoln's phrase, LWR's enterprises were to be "of the people" and "by the people" but, instead of "for the people" they were to be undertaken *with* the people. Like the rejection that is likely to accompany transplants of human organs, anything merely attempted for the people may fail to take into account local conditions and vital cultural factors. Jerry Aaker, one of the most perceptive workers in the development field, has summarized the resulting problem: "History reveals many examples of outside churches and organizations building up institutions, programs, and structures on their own terms and based on their own cultural orientations. When it is time to withdraw and turn it over to a national organization, things start getting complicated. Local leaders may fight over power and resources. Because of inappropriate structures and inadequate local capacity or willingness to assume something that is a foreign imposition, the transfer is fraught with problems." [1]

By contrast, projects undertaken by the people often generate a sense of ownership that promotes continuing involvement. In 1977, during the annual rainy season in northeast Brazil, severe floods washed out many dams but those built with the backing of Lutheran World Relief's partner agency, DIACONIA, were saved. When asked if he knew why, a DIACONIA staff member responded, "Of course! These were the people's dams. They stood guard over them 24 hours a day, calling out a work force to do sluicing whenever the water rose above the dam structure. The people had built those dams, they claimed ownership, and they weren't going to lose all they had." [2]

Even such food-for-work projects are limited by the fact that they are so dependent on outside resources, and often involve more workers temporarily than can be employed on the land made available by the project for cultivation. LWR has always tried to minimize these hazards in the selection of projects.

Of the People

Ideally, all development efforts, whether material or human, should be creations of the people. People are more likely to do something about "felt needs" than to be prodded into activities for which they are not motivated. All of us, however, have needs that may come to our attention only through exchange with other people. The poorest of the poor are certainly aware of the possible existence of underlying needs that may be brought to the surface by persons whom they respect. How to uncover those needs and assist communities in discovering workable ways to deal with them was an early objective in LWR's exploration of accompaniment.

Korean associates with LWR in Korean Church World Service helped in identifying Muk Dong, approximately 20 miles south of Seoul, as a promising village for community development. A young Korean trained for leadership in such work and his wife, a home economist, were sent there to live. With the help of local volunteers they built for themselves a simple house with an additional room to serve as a community center. Only the cost of construction materials and salary for the couple were to be provided from LWR. It was understood that nothing but what was already available to all Korean groups from local or national sources would be contributed for any projects. At first the couple made no attempt to initiate a development program but acquainted themselves with all of the villagers. They learned what interested the people and what they felt might improve life in Muk Dong. From these contacts they identified potential leaders to serve on a Community Development Committee whose members could develop a list of goals and priorities for later implementation.

When the first plans were ready, the entire community was assembled outdoors to consider them. Committee members reported on a wide range of goals, along with priorities for action. One man, proposing to inaugurate a family planning program, even confided that he had already undertaken to have a vasectomy and other village leaders had agreed to join him. Within 18 months residents of that village had made significant improvements in the agriculture, health, and education of the village. Chicks that grew into flocks of 50 laying hens were obtained for six households. The new "miracle rice" was introduced and the irrigation system for rice cultivation was improved. Plans were made to erect a mill to husk and polish the rice; an attempt to educate the villagers to use more unpolished rice encountered cultural resistance. A silkworm industry was initiated and mulberry trees were planted to provide the necessary food. One exception was made to the exclusion of foreign assistance when pedigreed dairy cattle were obtained from Heifer Project International to start a productive herd. A road was built to facilitate transport of commodities. Health of the village was improved by constructing a community bathhouse, adding indoor toilets to a number of homes, arranging for weekly visits by city doctors who volunteered their services, and instituting vaccination programs against common infectious diseases.

As the program expanded, it attracted the interest of friends in nearby villages, where similar projects were then undertaken entirely on local initiative. When Abner and Martha Batalden visited Muk Dong years later, long after LWR support had been discontinued, they found a rice mill busy and prospering, numerous houses rebuilt and enlarged, running water coming from a tank in the hills back of the village, an active nutrition-education program, quantities of vegetables in the town market, and a number of rapidly expanding agricultural programs. A sign on the roadway leading into the village indicated that the government of Korea had designated Muk Dong "The Model Community Development Village for the Eighties." [3]

Stages in Development

Muk Dong was a good example of emerging concepts of development in the seventies. Gradually more attention would be given to factors beyond local control. The economy of remote villages could not be isolated from the economy of a nation, or even the world. Communities on the margins of society could be squeezed out of markets that would have enabled their people to exchange goods and services beyond those they were able to provide for themselves. They lacked a voice in the dominant political systems of a nation.

Sobered by the enormous complexity of dealing with global hunger and poverty, development agencies experimented with different approaches to their tasks, and a progression of stages emerged.

The first stage, providing material assistance in times of crisis, was and is unavoidable. Christians, at least, cannot stand by and know that there are humans who are cold, hungry, or homeless. This was Lutheran World Relief's original purpose and is still characterized by the shipment of food, clothing, blankets, and medicine.

It was soon obvious that this was not enough. To prepare for the future it was necessary to help improve agriculture and conditions of health, nutrition, and sanitation. In many cases this could occur only with new access to water and with introduction of new crops and methods of farming. Roads were essential for marketing handicrafts and other products such as bricks, soap, silk, tiles, and bread. The second stage, then, concentrated on developing self-sufficient communities by sponsoring projects to improve local living conditions.

A third stage, or perhaps an aspect of the second, was concentration on developing individuals, especially leaders. Community planning was encouraged, along with literacy and various aspects of education. Women were assisted to prepare for expanded roles in the community and to engage in family planning.

Another stage recognized the limited prospects for single villages and contemplated means of helping to empower such communities to exert influence within their immediate political and social systems.

It took awhile for one more stage to be given major attention: mobilizing people not only in the poorer countries but, especially in the more affluent ones, to advocate changes in global relationships that would make better provision for economic and social justice.

Lutheran World Relief has not proceeded through these stages separately or sequentially. All have been undertaken in various combinations at different times, abbreviated in some cases and expanded in others. Even the need for advocacy was recognized from the beginning, as when LWR officials testified in Washington concerning government policy toward the world's poor. Thus the first stage, relief, was undertaken in conjunction with the final stage, global awareness.

Always Emergencies

Although Lutheran World Relief in the seventies emphasized participating in development efforts with the people, the relief aspect of its work, as in every decade, could not be neglected. The year 1970 was typical. In Yugoslavia 200,000 people were affected by extensive damage from the last of three earthquakes. Medicines valued at $53,281 and 2,480 blankets were channeled through the Yugoslav Red Cross. A major earthquake in Turkey killed 3,000 people and left

90,000 homeless. LWR shipped 192,607 pounds of clothing. When rain flooded twenty towns in Rumania, 170 victims died and 70,000 homes were either destroyed or badly damaged. LWR contributed $10,000 toward relief efforts organized by the World Council of Churches and the Lutheran World Federation. An unusually severe earthquake devastated 30,000 square miles in Peru, killing at least 50,000 people as whole mountainsides cascaded through villages, totally burying some. Lutheran World Relief responded immediately with 13,400 blankets and cash for purchase of emergency supplies. In the most devastating disaster of the decade, at least 228,000 residents of East Pakistan, later known as Bangladesh, were swept to their deaths in a hurricane that raced up the Bay of Bengal. Tidal waves 25 feet higher than normal, whipped by winds of 100 to 150 miles per hour, swept across the densely inhabited and deeply impoverished delta region. LWR response included 8,000 blankets and vaccine for 20,000 people. When millions of East Pakistani refugees came later to India, LWR contributed $100,000 for shelter, milk feeding programs, and occupational therapy, in addition to 2,000 tons of food, 90,000 blankets, plus clothing and soap. Lutheran World Relief played an equally significant role when the war ended and India shipped the refugees back in truckloads with no provisions to maintain themselves. LWR inaugurated an airlift to drop supplies, especially blankets warehoused in Calcutta.[4]

When the civil war in Nigeria ended in January, 1970, members of an LWR medical team already in the country were moved to the former Biafran capital of Owerri, the very center of the most critical need. Shipments of medicine and clothing were dispatched immediately. Soon Neil Brenden was employed by LWR to serve on the staff of the Commission on Relief and Rehabilitation of Nigeria's Christian Council and to administer a number of projects to aid in reconstruction and rehabilitation.[5]

In addition to Nigeria, other countries aided by LWR to deal with the suffering from wars and the results of wars included Bangladesh, Lebanon, Jordan, Vietnam, Ethiopia, Kampuchea (Cambodia), Nicaragua, Sudan, and Liberia.

During the rest of the seventies Lutheran World Relief continued to help many countries recover from "natural" catastrophes. Given on short notice, this aid was likely to reach the most needy because it was often administered through indigenous church agencies with knowledgeable personnel. In some cases LWR had already been active in the area, in other instances the Lutheran World Federation or Church World Service had local relationships.[6]

So, in the seventies, Lutheran World Relief did not neglect its initial function, and relief efforts kept hope alive for thousands of suffering people. Confronting disaster was sometimes a step toward development. In Nigeria, for example, relief was followed by assistance in improving agricultural production. Grants were made to establish 60 young future farmers on new farms and offer cultivating and marketing know-how; an 1,800-acre rural agricultural training center with outreach to numerous villages was established. Family planning and health clinics were included in the project.[7]

People who pulled together in an emergency were more ready to work together to improve their situation. Local leadership identified in a time of crisis could be encouraged to plan for the future. Wherever regional agencies gave promise of providing responsible direction for development efforts, Lutheran World Relief was supportive. In 1972, for example, when church leaders in Chile initiated a social welfare and development agency called DIACONIA, the name used elsewhere in Latin America, Lutheran World Relief assisted immediately in stockpiling emergency supplies as part of a disaster plan, but also in supporting a maternal and child nutrition health program, and in planning for self-help and development projects.

The hope that relief, supplemented by development assistance, could move a community toward self-sufficiency was reinforced when, at the end of 1971, Lutheran World Relief was able to end its support for projects in Korea. After 19 years of supplying personnel, funds, clothing, food, and medicines valued at more than $15 million, LWR could turn its responsibilities over to the appropriate service agency affiliated with the National Christian Council of Korea.[8]

There was no lack of opportunities to allocate the services that had been offered in Korea. Lutheran World Relief provided assistance to more than 50 countries in the seventies. A few received only relief, the rest either moved toward development or continued efforts already begun in that direction. Nearly every venture could provide a chapter in LWR's recorded history; these pages will allow only for selected examples.

Water as Lifeblood

The overwhelming need in parts of Africa, Asia, and Latin America was for food. A major obstacle to agricultural production in many areas was lack of water. Dams and irrigation systems were helpful in some places, but in others a more reliable, continuing source was needed. Lutheran World Relief took the lead in developing such a resource.

The country of Niger is not mentioned in LWR documents until 1974 and involvements were expanded significantly in later decades, but the basis for much of them was created soon after work was begun there. Niger is a Sahelian country, most of which lies within the Sahara Desert. In the southern areas, where subsistence farming is at least possible, severe droughts were experienced between 1968 and 1974. There were frequent crop failures, caused either by insufficient total rainfall during the rainy season, or poorly timed rainfall patterns. In many of those areas there was abundant water less than ten yards below the surface, but traditional, hand-dug wells were not satisfactory because the unstable, sandy soil caused them to collapse. Specialized teams using mechanized equipment could create workable wells but the cost was beyond the means of local gardeners. LWR took the initiative in developing a less expensive system that became standard throughout Niger. No mechanical lifting devices were required and concrete rings were cast in place and did not need to be lowered into the wells. Local teams were enlisted to spend two weeks learning to develop such a well; some of them learned to instruct others in the process and, in this way over a ten-year period, more than 3,000 wells were constructed.

The availability of a reliable water supply opened the gates for an impressive range of projects. In a number of villages seeds were provided, new vegetables and fruit trees were introduced, storage facilities were constructed, irrigation systems were developed, and roads were improved for better access to the region. Live fences, consisting of sturdy, bristling plants, were grown and maintained to protect gardens against destruction by animals. In some locations plows and cattle were acquired to work the heavy soils.

All of these material accomplishments were related to the development of individuals and communities. Education was an integral part of the experience. Each project was a venture of the people because there was such a pressing need for water. All of the work was done by the people and all of the planning was undertaken with the people. These plans often included provision for reimbursement of the cost of materials. Seeds, for example, were loaned at the beginning of a season and, after the harvest, reimbursement was expected. Such income was not returned to LWR but was allocated to a fund administered by the local cooperative to be used for future loans. Loans for other purposes were handled similarly both in Niger and elsewhere. Although there was not always repayment in full, the practice was continued as a caution against dependency and a reminder of the importance of individual responsibility[9].

Lutheran World Relief supported similar programs, combining agricultural and community development, in other African countries during the seventies. In an area of Togo known as "Kante Farm," provision for a reliable water supply made possible the growth of vegetables, grazing of cattle, and ponds for supplying protein-rich fish. Farmers learned to use the animals as an energy source and formed cooperatives to market their products and deal with government. In the Hurri Hills of Kenya a project also dealt with the familiar problem of an insufficient water supply. At Rumbeck in the Sudan an ox-plowing training center was established to help farmers raise food production from a mere subsistence level to cash crops. In Swaziland, where the economy was changing from a largely subsistence form to a semi-industrial society, a training center enabled students to produce pottery for sale. They learned how to build their own kilns, prepare clay, make pots, and glaze. The range of projects varied with local conditions and the resources of the area. In all cases there was every attempt to support only what was rooted in the community and could be undertaken by and with the residents.

Water from Rock

There were understandable similarities between Lutheran World Relief activities in Africa and Asia. There were many areas on both continents suffering from severe shortages of water. One of the more spectacular accomplishments in Asia involved a venture reminiscent of the Israelites being granted water from the rock at Horeb. Many U.S. Lutherans will remember seeing the film, *Miracle at Baramati.*

In Baramati County of Maharashtra State in India, there were 45 villages on rocky, barren land chronically in need of water. What little was available had to be carried from a canal two miles away. During the rare periods of rainfall the water quickly flowed away down 150 streams temporarily flowing through the area. Shallow wells were often dry, and deepening them appeared to be impossible because the strata of hard rock went to a depth of more than 100 feet. The situation seemed hopeless but two women, Australian missionaries who, between them, had 65 years of living in the county, would not allow the villagers to despair. There was reason to believe that if "percolation dams" could be constructed to retain the occasional flow from the streams, water could then trickle into the streams and become available for irrigation. Experts even claimed that the retention of water in the new reservoirs would raise the level of the surrounding wells. Project plans were submitted to the state government for consideration, but were thought to be technically unfeasible; no support was provided at that time.

The women collected evidence that the proposal had merit on the basis of experience elsewhere and brought the plan to the Church's Auxiliary for Social Action (CASA). As a partner with CASA, LWR was invited to assist with the project and agreed, first, to secure food from the U.S. government to make possible the building of the dams on a food-for-work basis. Huge dams were constructed, with 300 to 400 men and women working together on each one. With no machines and only simple tools, dirt and stones were gathered and carried to the site where they were built into a dam.

When 38 reservoirs had been created in this way and 20 more were under construction, it was apparent that expectations were being realized. Water was being fed into the soil for sub-irrigation and 40,000 acres of land were newly productive. Not only were the dams collecting water, but the water level had been raised until some wells were now usable. It became clear that if hundreds of additional wells could be dug, the rocky villages could be transformed. Digging them would not be easy because of the rock, but some drilling and blasting could make the project feasible. For this, money would be needed and LWR recognized an opportunity for significant participation in a rare venture. The cost for the first hundred wells was calculated at $137,500, and by this time officials of the government were so impressed with what was being accomplished that the Land Development Bank was willing to match whatever funds would be provided from other sources. Lutheran World Relief committed $67,500 to the fund and a separate agency, the Baramati Agricultural Development Trust, was formed to administer it and proceed with other development efforts. Each farmer needing a well was loaned $1,350, to be repaid to the fund over seven years, and thus to be available to others. The money was used to hire workers to assist in the digging, to pay for the blasting, and to buy a pump. Government engineers supervised the work.

While the wells were being sunk, additional dams were being built until they numbered more than 200 by the end of the decade. This

made it possible for more wells to become usable and U.S. government
funds became available for this next phase of the project.

As the water began flowing, the rocky area began to yield crops
of okra, jawar (a millet), onions, leeks, cabbage, pepper, beans,
cauliflower, and tomatoes. Cattle, sheep, goats, and chickens could be
raised. Within years, thousands of liters of milk were being exported
daily from Baramati. Sugar cane could be taken to the local mill by
ox cart. Land was set aside for a farm to be used for experimentation,
raising of seeds, and education of farmers through demonstration of
improved methods. Thousands of trees were planted and watered to
help reclaim what had been wasteland. Even fruit orchards were
grown.

Accomplishments at Baramati were impressive to people other
than government officials. Individuals both nearby and far away
became willing to assist people so devoted to becoming self-sufficient.
A German agency provided financial assistance, medicines, and two
mobile medical units, one for veterinary services. Doctors from the
nearest city volunteered to take turns staffing the dispensaries free of
charge. The vans ordinarily visited six villages and treated as many as
600 patients daily.

Improvement in their physical surroundings stimulated villagers to
develop their human potential. Many learned to read and write.
Young people crowded classes in which they could learn diversified
skills. Women were freed from some of their former drudgery, learned
to make many items for use in the home, and studied nutrition and
hygiene. Some achieved economic independence by producing items
for use by others. For thousands of people, what had happened at
Baramati was a miracle.[10]

Two other commitments in India illustrate the range of LWR
involvement. One project was administered by an agency known as
Christian Mission Service, founded by a German who settled in the
state of Tamil Nadu to devote his life to service as a Christian
layperson. Overall focus was on general agricultural development but
LWR support was channeled primarily to the establishment of a hostel
to accommodate 48 orphaned trainees. In India in the seventies there
were millions of orphans and thousands of orphanages, some of which
were unable to provide adequate care. Children from such institutions
were brought to the Glenbeck Agricultural Development Project where
they learned to raise cattle and cultivate the land during a three-year
training period. They also learned to participate in community
development activities, working beside the neighboring rural people.

Their labor and studies were directed toward preparing them for ultimate location elsewhere.[11]

Another venture initiated independently of Lutheran World Relief in 1970 began receiving LWR support in 1977. Drs. Rajanikant and (Mrs.) Mabelle Arole were determined to develop a low-cost, primary health system for the poorest and weakest sectors of the society. Their intention was to empower the people to manage their own affairs, not just in health but in every sector of their lives. For this purpose they established the Society for Comprehensive Rural Health Projects in Jamkhed, in one of the poorer regions of west-central India. Their holistic approach integrated health care with socio-economic development. LWR support enabled them to extend their work to a new project in Bhandardara. A later chapter of this book will report on subsequent evaluation of the Arole project, but already in 1979 they received the Magsaysay award, considered the Asian counterpart to the Nobel prizes.[12]

Latin America

Lutheran World Relief involvement in Latin America received increasing attention during the seventies. In addition to frequent emergency aid, development efforts were carried on in a number of countries. Brazil regularly received approximately two-thirds of the material assistance, but significant efforts were attempted in Nicaragua and Chile, among other locations. In Brazil LWR worked through DIACONIA, a social welfare and development agency of Protestant churches in the country. Much of LWR's assistance was devoted to familiar food-for-work projects, such as constructing dams, wells, reservoirs, irrigation canals, cesspools, roads, homes, and community centers. Technical help for food production was also offered, along with education for literacy, nutrition, and community development. Legal assistance provided advice for some of the poor whose land rights were threatened by illegal sales. Lutheran churches of the area made substantial contributions toward administrative and operational costs.[13]

An example of a venture with especially clear local roots was the Indian River Project in Limon, Nicaragua. Out of a strong sense of community and identity, leaders of the Sumu and Miskito Indians had been struggling with their people to raise their subsistence and living standard. They appealed for help to LWR's Nicaraguan partner agency, the Evangelical Committee for Development Assistance (CEPAD), and

LWR was able to respond. Many of the Sumus and Miskitos learned to read and write, and to produce more from their fields through improved tools and seeds. A preventative and curative health care system was developed. The indigenous people improved transportation through new roads and communication through their own publication. They studied how to obtain legal title to Indian territory which had belonged to their ancestors.[14]

In the Andean region of South America an LWR staff worker, Hans Hoyer, encouraged groups to talk with one another about their own needs and fully participate in planning and carrying out their own projects. Drawing on a modest development fund, Hoyer in 1979 helped trigger nearly two dozen projects. Each dollar from the fund generated five dollars' worth of local support in cash or labor. Skills such as cheesemaking were acquired, cooperatives were activated, and preventative health services were undertaken.[15]

Appropriate Technology

In all of the agency's innovative ventures, LWR representatives try to avoid recommending inappropriate technology. Marvelous inventions and methods that work well in one part of the world may be useless in another. In the highlands of Bolivia, installation of windmills seemed to be an obvious solution to the need for electricity. The idea proved to be unworkable, however, because of the difficulty and expense of bringing steel to the site.

LWR representatives in the seventies tried to distinguish between devices that were not adaptable to a particular situation and those that could contribute to the development process. In many locations oxen were more appropriate than tractors; the villagers knew how to employ them, they did not need complicated maintenance, and they did not cause unemployment. In one Bangladesh town a "factory" was even organized to create, by hand, wheels for ox carts, thus creating instead of destroying jobs. In the northern region of Cameroon, however, LWR supported a project to make available three small, self-help tractors, to the Evangelical Lutheran Church of the Cameroon, for use by farmers in six districts. Storage buildings with workshops were built with local labor. A pool of mechanics was already available from a vocational training center but additional Cameroonian tractor drivers/mechanics were trained. Government units cooperated. The tractors were loaned to the church, with farmers expected to pay for the plowing from their increased income, thus making possible the purchase of additional tractors. Each tractor was capable of doing the work of six oxen.

To protect crops from destruction by insects, westerners are likely to resort to chemical spraying, generally by air, but in the Sahelian zone of Africa a different strategy was employed. Date palm groves, supplying an important source of carbohydrates, calcium, and vitamin B for a famine-ravaged area, were threatened by a destructive insect. Since ladybugs were known to feed on that insect, Lutheran World Relief set aside $16,000 in 1973 to purchase enough ladybugs to devour the invaders. The ladybugs were incubated in net-enclosed palm trees. When they reached maturity they were released in infested groves, where each bug ate as many as 400 insects a day. The cost of the entire project was closer to $40,000 because an entomologist, equipped with a pickup truck and a portable laboratory, was employed to travel 18,000 miles per month to check on the disease and the bugs.

Irrigation pumps can be as expensive as they are important. An agricultural specialist employed by Lutheran World Relief, however, devised a method of adapting a pump to function in the rice paddies of Vietnam with locally available material costing three dollars. The adaptations of the pump could be completed in one day by a worker using simple tools. The inexpensive, lightweight pump was so efficient that it was soon being manufactured locally with support from South Vietnamese provincial authorities and the U.S. AID.[16]

Personal Impact

Lutheran World Relief's global services in the seventies were impressive. The value of annual investments of cash and material resources averaged more than $9 million. Huge areas of land were made available for cultivation. Local food supplies were increased in hundreds of locations. Estimates indicated that more than a million people were served annually, in one way or another. Above all, however, hope was restored in the lives of individuals, and this cannot be communicated through statistics. Only their stories convey the real impact of Lutheran World Relief's ministry.

In war-torn Vietnam 16-year-old Mi Bin survived the ravages of disease and death but faced an uncertain future until she began studying public health at a provincial hospital. Under the supervision of Ursula Horn, a nurse supplied by LWR to Vietnam Christian Service, she helped in makeshift clinics to administer inoculations and other elementary medical services, promote sanitation, and show how to plant more nutritious fruits and vegetables. Prepared to teach what she learned, Mi Bin could see how her life could make a difference.

In Brazil Dona Ralmunda was accustomed to going to the river bank to scrub and pound laundry on the rocks, spreading disease. The agency, DIACONIA, with LWR support, helped her community build a laundry with washtubs, ironing facilities, and bathrooms. Water could be filtered and the labor made easier. Dona Ralmunda soon was able to do enough laundry to earn income.

In Niger Riscoa Moussale had suffered from a long drought. His family's cattle perished and his father was fatally bitten by a snake in the desert. Riscoa had lost direction and hope. Then one day he saw a team of workers supported by Lutheran World Relief digging a shallow, low-cost well. This struck him as so important that he was eager to learn how to do it himself. He not only acquired the skill but became a trainer and taught dozens of villagers how to build wells easily with local materials. His own life was turned around.

A Minnesota farmer, Donald Sandager, sent by LWR to the Sudan, encouraged a local farmer with two acres of land to plant, for the first time, a packet of cabbage seeds. To the surprise of the Sudanese, 1500 cabbage heads were harvested. His profit was nearly 14 times more than the average Sudanese made in a year.

In Bangladesh 14-year-old Kamala was left behind when villagers of Mymensin fled from invading enemy soldiers. During the occupation she was raped repeatedly by a captain. When the village was liberated, custom decreed that "disgraced women" could not return to their homes. After many months Kamala was accepted in a hostel in the capital city of Dacca, where she entered the Women's Career Training Institute. A social worker provided by Lutheran World Relief, Colleen DuBois, helped Kamala to gain skills and courage to face a new life. She learned tailoring to qualify for a position in a factory set up to employ persons who had suffered such experiences. She was actually able to smile again.[17]

Accompanists

Colleen Du Bois, Donald Sandager, Ursula Horn, and Hans Hoyer, all were members of the unofficial Hope Corps, working in accordance with the Lutheran World Relief policy of accompaniment. LWR's development services in the seventies involved an increasing number of expatriates, most of whom will go unmentioned in the limited space of these pages. Between 20 and 30 people were usually representing

LWR in ،a dozen or so countries, with specialties ranging from mechanics to surgery. In theory their role was clear. Instead of taking charge of projects they were to "accompany" the poor in their striving for a more abundant life. To do this required gaining the respect of the people with whom they were working.

Most expatriates in service abroad begin by admitting that it will be impossible for them to identify so completely with the poor that they will be accepted without reservation and become fully qualified to reflect local attitudes. There are always exceptions: a few missionaries who spend their lives in one locale and become totally absorbed in the local culture. LWR field workers, however, usually spend only a few years in one place; it is not even economically wise for them to stay longer because part of their task is to empower locals to replace expatriates, which makes sense from the perspectives of both economy and development strategy.

This does not mean that accompanists cannot develop a very deep empathy with the people surrounding them. Martha Batalden, who worked beside her husband in Korea, Vietnam, India, and Bangladesh, commented that Americans who heard about their experiences sometimes said to her, "I suppose you get used to the poverty." But Martha contended, "That's a terrible thing to say. You never get used to it." [18]

But the expatriate must always sense his or her limitations and work within them. Jerry Aaker, who served LWR in Vietnam and in many Latin American communities, has questioned the appropriateness of programs where foreigners try to work directly at the local level. His experience convinced him that his "job as an outsider was not directly with the poor at the grassroots." Instead, he concluded, "In order to understand and empathize with the plight of the poor, it was necessary to constantly visit projects and community leaders, talk with campesinos (peasants), community leaders, and urban dwellers, and try to listen to their needs and ideas." In his opinion all foreigners should work with a local counterpart, underlining the principle that all LWR programs are ventures of, by, and with the people. Not incidentally, the counterpart is in a position to exercise more authority than an expatriate. In one community in Peru nearly all farmers were enlisted by a strong, young local leader to participate in an agricultural project. When the leader's father refused, the father was jailed by his son for three days, causing laughter in the community. [19]

Coordinating the Complexity

In the seventies Lutheran World Relief had become engaged in so many different services in so many different localities that there was need for more coordination, evaluation, planning, and recruiting than could possibly be accomplished by a skeleton staff.

A few accompanists were brought into New York or regional offices to apply what they had learned to the overall planning process. Larry Roth, who had served in Vietnam and Cameroon after teaching in Guinea, moved into the central offices in 1974. Charles Fluegel, who had been a missionary in Madagascar, joined the New York staff in 1976. Gene Thiemann was brought from Africa to become director of interpretation in 1976. Hans Hoyer, a native of Germany with previous experience in Latin America, became LWR's first field-based regional consultant when, in 1979, he was placed in Lima, Peru, to "build bridges" among the various local institutions and international assistance agencies in Ecuador, Bolivia, Chile, and Peru. The movement of people was accelerated in the next decade.

Accompanists had a distinctive contribution to make to Lutheran World Relief efforts at home. Persons with "on the spot" experience could interpret the work and promote it with special effectiveness. They were also qualified to speak with credibility concerning U.S. policies toward the world's poor.

Along with the returning accompanists there was always a loyal coordinating staff in the New York office, bolstering the work of Bernard Confer and his executive assistant, Ove Nielsen. James Patterson, another executive assistant, retired in 1973 after ten years with LWR. In addition to dealing with financial and budgetary matters, he had supervised program activities in Latin America and the Middle East. George Matzat worked closely with Nielsen from 1971 to 1975 and had special responsibilities for program promotion. Candace Sadler completed 13 years of work as administrative assistant in 1972. Sheila Kammerer replaced her and continued in office until 1985. J. Robert Busche, who had been closely related to Lutheran World Relief while previously on the staffs of the National Lutheran Council and LCUSA, became an assistant executive secretary in 1973.

Important steps in the leadership of two domestic ventures occurred in 1975. It had become obvious that monitoring legislation and public policy concerning world hunger required diligent attention. A Washington presence was also needed to try to make U.S. policy more responsive to the needs of the poor and powerless in countries of the south. Since the requirements of Lutheran World Relief and Church World Service were so similar in this respect, the two agencies decided to cooperate in the funding of the Office on Development Policy, with 60% provided by CWS and 40% by LWR. Larry Minear was the first professional staff person employed and Carol Capps became his assistant in 1979.[20]

The other domestic venture with staffing expansion in the seventies provided support for projects that had been contributing significantly to LWR services. From the beginning Lutheran women especially had been contributing time, skill, and money toward the creation, collection, and shipping of clothing, quilts, soap, layettes, and Kiddies Kits. New York administrators had always encouraged these efforts but there was little staff time available for providing assistance and promotion. Details will be reported in the next chapter, but this part of LWR's work became recognized as a vital base for congregational contact and an important source of financial contributions. Alice Smith was the first staff person to have special projects as her responsibility and, after she retired in 1974, the activities were divided into parish projects with Edna Wagschal in charge, and special gifts under Betty Nute's direction.

End of an Era

Along with staff additions there were changes in membership on the LWR Board of Directors. Some were routine, recognizing aging of members or a shift in responsibilities to their church bodies. One notable step was the election of the first woman, Marie Sump of the Lutheran Church—Missouri Synod, to membership in 1976.

In 1970, a quarter of a century after LWR's formation, two of the five original directors were still in office. Two years later Michael Markel resigned and, in 1979, Paul Empie died. Within two years Bernard Confer, at the center of LWR's work since 1946, would retire. An era was ending.

Markel and Empie had contributed enormously to the mission of Lutheran World Relief. Markel was noted for his special insights and his wise counsel in deliberations dealing with complex problems. He had provided legal service to the National Lutheran Council, Lutheran Refugee Services, and Lutheran Film Associates, in addition to LWR.

Paul Empie's death represented more than the end of a presidential term. In some ways he was the most influential of all the early policy-makers of Lutheran World Relief. Because he was not only the

LWR president, but for many years the chief executive of the National Lutheran Council and, later, Lutheran World Ministries, companion agencies with offices in the same building, he was available for regular consultation with LWR staff members. Bernard Confer said he was "more knowledgeable than any other person about conditions within Lutheranism around the world, and particularly on their service programming." [21]

Empie was warm in personal relationships but could also be professionally demanding. Once when Confer wrote Ove Nielsen from abroad, instructing him to include Brazil on the agenda for the next board meeting, Nielsen went to Empie to clear the matter with the president, and was challenged immediately with a series of six questions, all relevant to the proposal. Flabbergasted by having failed to anticipate such a response, Nielsen on the next day, Saturday, borrowed three library books on Brazil. He read them by Sunday evening and had a memorandum on Empie's desk by Monday morning, answering the six questions. Empie phoned him saying, "I see that you know more about Brazil than you knew Friday." He supported the project when it was presented. [22]

Empie devoted large blocks of time to speaking on behalf of Lutheran World Relief. His passion for the global needs was a part of his heritage, as he explained in at least one of his addresses. One of his earliest memories of childhood was waking up and hearing sharp voices downstairs. His beloved grandmother was criticizing her son-in-law, Empie's father, for failing to give his wife enough of an allowance to dress decently. At that time his father's salary for a family of seven was $1,200 a year, but he said this to his mother-in-law, "Now mother, you're welcome in this home anytime you want to come, but you can't tell me how to run my family. I give Grace all I can spare for clothes, according to what I have. Do you know what she does with it? She gives it all to foreign missions, and patches her old dresses. Do you think I'm going to get her to stop that?" Empie then asked his listeners bluntly whether anyone who really cared to the point of sacrifice like that could settle for giving a dollar a year for needs abroad. This was the approximate amount appropriated for relief purposes through synodical budgets. [23]

Until his death Empie continued to push for more reliable sources of financial support for relief and development, a concern that received special consideration in the seventies.

Support from Church and State

Staff concern for the financing of LWR projects was understandable. U.S. policy was always subject to change. In the sixties income from the church bodies had increased only modestly. At the beginning of the decade, when the two new churches, The American Lutheran Church and the Lutheran Church in America, made LWA-LWR funds a budget item, allocations actually declined for several years, staying close to $500,000. Later there were increases and The Lutheran Church—Missouri Synod brought its contribution into line with its proportionate membership, approximately half of the total of the other two. The Wisconsin Synod continued to contribute for special projects. By the beginning of the seventies LWR annual income from those official sources had reached a million dollars. There was little change in the total for several years.

This was not nearly enough for crisis relief in addition to development efforts. When special appeals, approved to deal with the Nigeria-Biafra conflict, raised more than a million dollars, it was obvious that Lutherans were willing and eager to contribute more for service to the world's needy than could be raised through existing channels. Media coverage of crushing droughts in Africa in 1974 also brought great pressure on church bodies to act.

Appeals Outside the Budgets

The Lutheran Church—Missouri Synod was the first of the bodies to take official action to remedy the situation. Steps were taken to carry out the intention of the 1969 resolution reported in chapter 6, "To Intensify Efforts to Alleviate World Hunger." A Commission on World Hunger was created to work closely with the LCMS Board of World Relief. The World Relief office was moved from the Detroit area to St. Louis to strengthen coordination with all LCMS units. In 1971 LCMS congregations were urged to begin observing an annual World Relief/World Hunger Sunday. In 1973 the Synod established a goal of a million dollars for dealing with overseas hunger. From the beginning LCMS maintained a connection between domestic and overseas concerns. While cooperating with LWR, LCMS also undertook some overseas efforts independently, especially those connected with LCMS missions.

The theological and bureaucratic turbulence within the Lutheran Church—Missouri Synod during the seventies, resulting eventually in the separation of more than 200 congregations and the formation of the Association of Evangelical Lutheran Churches, did not materially affect LCMS participation in LWR. Leslie F. Weber, who had been director of the Board of Social Ministry when that agency was merged with the LCMS Board of World Relief, became a member of the LWR Board in 1971 and later explained that LCMS increased its support each year, believing "that LWR is doing a great job in human needs, not just in responding to emergencies, but also in helping to prevent some of those difficulties from happening." Weber agreed with the LWR policy of serving on the basis of need, not creed, explaining, "This is the way that our Savior distributed his relief. The 5,000 fed were not all Christians; distribution was not conditional." [1] Melvin E. Witt, who became LCMS Secretary of World Relief in 1972, observed that the Synod's World Relief/World Hunger Appeal was supported by all factions within the LCMS.[2]

The Lutheran Church in America issued periodic statements concerning hunger and poverty before establishing, in 1974, a world hunger appeal. Initial authorization was for only two years, but included references beyond relief to development focused on endemic need, sensitizing the constituency, and supporting governmental programs.

In The American Lutheran Church hunger and poverty also received regular attention in official gatherings, especially stimulated by the youth, but it was also 1974 before a special hunger appeal was begun. Thanksgiving was designated as the time for the ingathering and a Committee on World Hunger was established to plan for the effort.

The special appeals had an immediate impact on funding for Lutheran World Relief. By the middle of the decade more than a million dollars came annually from world hunger sources and this amount doubled by the end of the seventies, exceeding the regularly budgeted income from the church bodies.[3] The surge was stimulated in 1979 by the massive tragedy in Cambodia, where it was estimated that up to half of the seven million population had been lost and most of the rest were on the edge of starvation.

The appeals begun in the seventies raised the sights for many local congregations. In 1975 Grace Lutheran Church in Des Moines,

Washington, resolved to raise a million dollars in response to world hunger by the end of the century. After reaching that goal in 1993, seven years early, the congregation has continued to raise $70,000 each year for the same purpose.

In all three national church bodies the appeals, initially established as immediate responses to particular crises, found permanent lodging within the organizational structures, with provision for responsible staff. The AELC had hunger appeals from the beginning and continued them until the merger with the ALC and LCA into the Evangelical Lutheran Church in America.

From the midseventies there has been coordination in the operation of the appeals in all four of the church bodies, including LCMS. The story of this significant ministry is reported in the book by Charles P. Lutz, *Loving Neighbors Far and Near: U.S. Lutherans Respond to a Hungry World.*[4]

Solid Base

One source of LWR support, donations of clothing, quilts, blankets, soap, and kits, remained strong after more than a quarter of a century. In 1972 Lutheran groups and individuals contributed 154,200 blankets or quilts; sewed 8,100 items of clothing for Africa and the Middle East, plus 8,000 pajama-like garments for Vietnam; assembled 13,400 layettes, 19,900 Klenli-Kits for assistance in health care and 17,700 Activiti-Kits with learning tools for children; and donated 205,100 pounds of soap. Altogether, LWR received 3,074,000 pounds of goods for use abroad.

References to this program in previous chapters have only touched on the depth of commitment represented by this aspect of LWR's outreach. Members of women's organizations from all of the churches associated with LWR were the principal contributors; thousands of women met regularly to sew, dedicating their time and ability, as well as money, to the needs of the poor. After a few years most of the blankets shipped abroad were actually quilts, the creation of which gave the women a special sense of identification with the persons who would eventually be warmed and sheltered. Some of the quilts were sewn at home by women willing to devote more than a few hours weekly to the project.

There were women who set goals for themselves, such as completing a quilt each week, or 52 per year. Ada Leffert, for example, from Mendota, Illinois, in 1974 at nearly 70 years of age, resolved to make 50 quilts a year until she completed 1000. She reached her goal in 1994.[5]

Ruth Helling from Seattle, Washington, began earlier, in 1967, to make quilts at home and averaged 52 a year thereafter. She and her husband, Ken, became deeply involved in another part of the shipment program in 1974, when they were given charge of the gathering and shipping of clothing and quilts for LWR in the northwest Washington area. Along with volunteers from Spokane and Seattle, they began coordinating the loading of donations twice a year, in May and November. Originally all goods were loaded onto boxcars, but when railroad trailers replaced them the operation was moved to the parking lot of Our Redeemer's Lutheran Church in Seattle. More distant churches centralized their collections and delivered them to the loading site by rental truck. LWR was responsible for transporting the donations to a warehouse in Maryland, but many of the participating congregations and individuals contributed to the shipping costs. Within 13 years after the Hellings took charge, shipments increased from 20 to 100 tons. The Hellings have been quick to give full credit for the program to Lutheran women, but they have encouraged participation by distributing, at their own expense, a quarterly LWR newsletter to 900 congregations and individuals in the Pacific Northwest. The newsletter has featured information about loadings, the items needed, and the work of LWR. The Hellings' home congregation, Queen Anne Lutheran Church in Seattle, has provided a base for their operations.[6]

Many other volunteers have devoted huge blocks of time and effort to the shipping efforts of LWR. Kenneth and Muriel Greene, from Tescott, Kansas, have traveled across the state and even beyond, gathering donations in a big truck.[7] Ordinarily as many as 80 key leaders have organized the regional appeals.

Ken Helling and Kenneth Greene's roles are reminders that women have not been the only contributors to the sewing and shipping program. At least one man, Clair Kloster of Decorah, Iowa, has not been fazed by the sewing records of women and has reached a production level of nearly 80 quilts annually. At age 82, he made almost 400 quilts in less than six years prior to 1995.

Many male pastors have been instrumental in educating congregations concerning the opportunities for service offered by Lutheran World Relief. One pastor and veteran promoter of LWR, George William (Bill) Genszler, became known as "The Blanket Man."

He regularly inspired Lutherans from Wisconsin and Michigan to contribute record amounts of quilts, blankets, and clothing. In 1976 he completed 25 years of this devoted service and continued his efforts for many years prior to his death in 1993. He was also instrumental in encouraging the Siebert Foundation of Milwaukee, Wisconsin, to make annual contributions of $20,000 over a long period of time to cover the cost of inland transporting for the Wisconsin collections.

While leading regional appeals in the seventies, Genszler reflected LWR's growing emphasis on development when he said, "To those who know the love of Christ, relief must blossom into new patterns of enduring love. The love of the Good Samaritan is the Lord's example of such a love. It began with relief on the Jericho Road but continued to make provision for the victim's well-being on the morrow." Expressing his own commitment, Genszler said, "I love Lutheran World Relief because its creative, enduring concern is giving tens of thousands 'a crack at life.' To me LWR means Lutheran World Re-Life." [8]

People engaged in sewing were reminded by LWR staff that their creations often led to more than momentary relief. Layettes could be distributed in connection with prenatal classes that included study of child care and family planning. School kits could encourage attendance at literacy classes. Health kits and soap contributed to concern for family health. A sewing kit made it possible for someone to learn dressmaking.

Occasional specialized appeals also alerted women to particular needs and opportunities. In 1972 a space filler in *Scope*, national magazine for women of The American Lutheran Church, suggested that if every subscriber gave a quarter, $80,000 could be raised for Bangladesh. Readers were informed that $55 would build a house in Bangladesh, $25 could buy an ox for plowing, and $30 would provide a well for drinking water. Thousands of women sent quarters but hundreds also added checks. One woman sent $110, saying that $55 was for building a house, noting that her "small, very modest" home cost more than that; $25 was for an ox, with the comment that she didn't have an ox but a 10-year-old car that "runs well with occasional first aid"; and $30 was for a well, realizing that she had only to turn a faucet for water.[9] Such experiences supported the conviction that many Lutherans would give additional support to LWR efforts if approached directly.

The involvement by Lutheran women's organizations in collecting material resources for shipping was also an important element in the education of congregations. In some localities it became traditional to gather and display quilts made by members on a particular Sunday each year, when the worship service would center around global needs. The resulting inspiration and consciousness-raising has been important for both worshipers and LWR. Later, groups of women began visiting overseas locations of LWR work, qualifying them to report personally concerning the impact of the services rendered.

Reviewing the Strategy

Efforts in the seventies to increase financial support from the churches for an expanding Lutheran World Relief naturally led to thoughtful examination of the basis for the whole endeavor. In 1972 revisions were made in the LWR Certificate of Incorporation, recognizing changes in effect since 1945. A reference to "war-created needs" was deleted and recognition was inserted of "projects to help needy people to help themselves." Instead of citing "the countries of continental Europe," the territory of operation was broadened to include countries with "a need for relief."

A more extensive study explored an overall strategy to deal with world hunger. The policy statement adopted a decade earlier, reported in chapter 6, needed updating and sharpening. LWR ventures had already gone beyond the expectations of that document, but needs were increasing at a faster rate. World population and food supply were badly out of balance. According to one projection, within ten years there would be a surplus of 51.9 million tons of food in developed nations and a deficit of 47.6 million tons in developing countries. Development efforts thus far had not prevented this gap from growing. What direction should be taken by Lutheran World Relief to address this problem?

From the staff, Ove Nielsen and Robert Busche prepared an initial document for consideration by the board. It was a comprehensive review of the global need and LWR's potential capability for addressing it. Lutheran World Relief had already taken steps to reflect a new development theory, locally oriented, involving only small amounts of capital, focused on empowerment of local individuals and institutions. What guidelines could be adopted to give this theory more expression?

The draft was submitted to the board and also circulated among representatives of other voluntary agencies and, after all reactions were considered, a revision was undertaken by Larry Roth and adopted by the board. The result included some principles familiar to readers of previous chapters of this book, but they were put into a framework of nine categories, each of which was accompanied by specific principles for implementation. Following are the nine categories in the list of *Lutheran World Relief Development Strategy Guidelines*:

1. Project ideas must originate in the target group.
2. Projects should serve the poorest majority.
3. The political, social, and economic implications of the projects should work in the favor of the ultimate well-being of the target group.
4. Projects should stimulate development of the national and local structures, enabling them to identify problems, plan solutions, and organize work.
5. Projects should use indigenous human and material resources as much as possible.
6. Project activities should become self-supporting.
7. Projects should be technically sound.
8. Individual project activities should be integrated into a comprehensive program.
9. Projects must be reviewed and evaluated periodically.[10]

The adoption of so comprehensive a strategy led to one of many board discussions concerning the accuracy of the name, Lutheran World Relief. Now that the agency was expanding its efforts so far beyond relief alone, should a more descriptive name be adopted? Then, as later, no action was taken. Suggested options conflicted with titles of other agencies. Directors also feared that a new name would only add to existing confusion; Lutherans already had trouble distinguishing among LWR, LWA, LWF, and LWM, plus NLC and LCUSA. Lutheran World Relief had earned a reputation for service, stewardship, and integrity that made the name worth retaining.

In deliberating over provisions of the strategy, members of the staff and board were always aware that LWR efforts were only part of a much larger whole. Governmental actions played a critical role in dealing with world hunger. Policies were crucial, but money was not incidental. Even in financial terms, the value of commodities channeled through LWR during the first 25 years by U.S. government agencies constituted approximately half of LWR's total expenditures. Looking to future support, Lutheran World Relief had to give attention to support from state as well as church.

Fluctuating State Support

U.S. administrations from the time of Harry Truman generally favored granting substantial assistance to nations in need. Members of congress were often less supportive, fearing opposition from voters conditioned to oppose anything described as foreign aid.

During President Kennedy's tenure, the Peace Corps and the American Freedom from Hunger Foundation had been created. A number of organizations were combined into the U.S. Agency for International Development (AID).

Richard Nixon in 1970 took a number of positions concerning U.S. foreign assistance that were welcomed by Confer and, on his recommendation, commended by LWR directors. The president had expressed his conviction that the foundation for such aid should "be a partnership among the nations in pursuit of a truly international development effort." This appealed to Confer, who believed it "unrealistic to expect other nations to support programs molded by Americans." Nixon's proposal to separate security assistance from relief and development assistance was applauded by Confer, who observed that "perhaps the least efficient aid programs have been those which have been tied most closely to security positions, as in Vietnam." Nixon even advocated that "all donor countries take steps to end the requirement that foreign aid be used to purchase goods and services in the nation providing the aid," something strongly favored by LWR on the grounds that "frequently dollar aid would have covered more goods and services if they were secured in a country other than the United States." While responding to the presidential positions, the LWR Board of Directors noted the increase in hunger and poverty around the world and urged "the government to increase substantially the amount of funds it devotes to overseas social and economic development." [11]

Nixon's experience in dealing with reluctance from some administrators and members of Congress concerning foreign assistance resulted in a spotty record, similar to those of his predecessors and successors.

In 1973 the U.S. government announced that no food would be available under PL 480, the Food for Peace Program, for shipment from October through December. This was the first time in 19 years that such drastic action had been taken. There had been major crop failure in areas of Russia, China, and West Africa, causing such a demand in the purchasing of food that less could be classified as surplus. As a result, however, thousands of people suffering from famine had no access to food.[12] LWR participated in protesting to Congress and shipping was restored in 1974, but the experience highlighted the fragility of government support and stimulated LWR staff to give more attention to U.S. policy.

From Reaction to Initiative

Lutheran World Relief had never been hesitant to react to government policy, actions, or inaction. Even while receiving assistance, LWR had expressed reservations about the relationship between a religious agency and the state, as when caution was expressed lest the voluntary agency lose its independence. There was also concern over a dilemma that could arise from assisting a program established on a government-to-government basis. If experience pointed to a need for change in the political or social structures of the indigenous government participating in such an arrangement, there would be even less opportunity than usual to facilitate or even advocate such change.

In 1973 Confer testified before a Senate committee that LWR favored lifting the prohibition against selling government food commodities to countries such as North Vietnam. He reported that his agency had gone on record as saying that, in view of the nation's abundant agricultural productivity, "food really should be removed from the political arena; Americans should be concerned with the hungry wherever they may be." [13]

LWR staff members and policy makers had become convinced that determining their own strategy was not enough. Their LWR ventures were affected in many significant ways by government policy, and their years of experience qualified them to evaluate government practices. While clarifying LWR objectives, then, they saw the need for changes in national policy and decided to express their conclusions in the form of a document, "Toward the Development of a United States Food Policy." Robert Busche and Ove Nielsen undertook this writing also.

In the preparation of such a comprehensive statement, experts from around the world were consulted and relevant documents considered. LWR joined in the formation of a broad coalition of religious and secular groups to prepare for the 1974 World Food Conference in Rome. Other religious agencies in this World Hunger Coalition were Church World Service, Catholic Relief Services, Church Women United, and Crusade Against Hunger. Secular organizations participating ranged from the National Farmers' Union to the American Council of Voluntary Agencies for Foreign Service.[14]

The statement that emerged from the study and was adopted by the board in 1974 began by calling attention to the "very real possibility" that death from starvation "could strike down more people in a single year than were killed in World Wars I and II." Factors pointing in this direction were cited: the dangerous dwindling of the world's food reserve; the likelihood of severe droughts predicted by meteorologists and resulting from change in the world's climate; increasing consumption of food, fuel and other resources by affluent nations at the expense of poorer countries. The cause for emphasizing these concerns at that particular time lay in the U.S. action reducing availability of food under the Food for Peace Program.

Lutheran World Relief therefore called for prompt action by the U.S. Government to address this problem, encouraging the adoption of eleven specific policies:

1. Commit annually at least 10% of food grains available for export for use in programs of humanitarian assistance.
2. Insure the use of such food on the basis of need without discrimination in order that food not be used as a political tool.
3. Encourage maximum agricultural production in the U.S.
4. Establish multi-year commitments to enhance sound planning.
5. Support development of an international network of food reserves.

6. Increase support for the United Nations Children's Emergency Fund, the Food and Agriculture Organization, and the World Food Program.
7. Establish safeguards against extreme fluctuations of agricultural commodity prices which might place disproportionate responsibility and risk upon the U.S. farmer.
8. Enlist the support of other nations in assisting the poor.
9. Encourage citizens' initiatives in reducing wasteful and excessive use of food, fuel, and fertilizer.
10. Provide for the establishment of economic relations and mechanisms to achieve more effective production and more equitable distribution of food.
11. Support and stimulate research for discovering and developing new food resources and for increasing food production through husbandry of the sea.[15]

Direct Contact with Washington

It was soon after this document had been adopted that Larry Minear became the representative for both Lutheran World Relief and Church World Service in Washington. He began immediately to provide valuable information concerning applications of the policies to specific situations. When, for example, reports reached him that the State Department was preparing to monitor votes in the United Nations by countries receiving U.S. food aid, presumably to enable the U.S. to put pressure on certain countries by threatening to withhold such aid, LWR registered its protest to Secretary of State Henry Kissinger. The letter stated that such a policy would "hold human lives hostage, penalizing hungry people for the actions of their governments." The policy was criticized as "unworthy of a great nation with a broad vision, a generous spirit and a moral commitment to do what is right as a responsible partner in a hungry world." The letter urged "that the use of food aid as a political weapon be banished forever from the vocabulary and practice of U.S. diplomacy." [16]

Minear encouraged LWR to continue giving attention to national food policy, and the board in 1977 adopted a new resolution that reflected many of the same concerns expressed earlier. Several recommendations expanded provisions from 1974. A growing partnership was advocated "between government and voluntary agencies whose past performance and history of overseas service reflect competence and integrity, with provision to insure that the unique strengths of the voluntary agency community are safeguarded." New policies were to include "the responsible utilization of food aid and development assistance to facilitate the realization of the self-development and the self-reliance of needy nations, at the same time forswearing their use to achieve the short-term political objectives of the United States." Congress and a newly elected administration were urged to fashion a "comprehensive U.S. policy which recognizes the needs of chronic food-deficit nations not only for food but also for greater agricultural self-sufficiency, not only for aid but also for trade." The need for higher levels of development assistance was emphasized.[17]

At the same meeting when the new resolution on national policy was adopted by LWR, the board recommended normalizing relationships between the United States and Vietnam, and granting Vietnam membership in the United Nations. LWR staff members saw little possibility for carrying out substantial aid programs in the war-torn country until there was diplomatic recognition of Vietnam by the U.S. A related recommendation called for the removal of trade embargoes which were "hampering commercial relationships between private enterprise" in the two countries.[18]

Minear was given an opportunity for more direct input to national policy considerations when, in 1977, he was invited to serve on a White House staff team helping to develop options for newly elected Jimmy Carter's presidential initiative on world hunger. The team included three other consultants from private agencies, along with staff members from the Agency for International Development and the Department of Agriculture. The group was responsible for recommending both policy and specific actions in five areas of government involvement: food production and consumption in developing countries, research and technical cooperation with other nations, food reserves, food aid, and trade and investments.[19]

Prospects for Additional Government Support

While serving on the White House team, Minear was in a good position to evaluate prospects for government support of global aid and development efforts at the end of the seventies. In general he anticipated greater national concentration on "the poorest of the poor" and increased attention to the role of private voluntary agencies. He could identify some specific pluses and minuses. On the plus side he expected major policy changes to "make development assistance programs more thoroughly humanitarian and developmental." He expected increased tonnage of surplus commodities under a "food for development" label to be available to agencies such as LWR. A bilateral assistance program with India, broken off several years before, was to be resumed. A multi-year development effort in the drought-stricken Sahel area of Africa had been given congressional approval. Minear also noted improvement in food storage policies, some increases in price support levels, and the designation of larger amounts of funds for international development efforts.

On the minus side of his report card Minear saw a "politicization of development assistance to a new degree," reflecting a protectionist mood in Congress. The World Bank and similar institutions were under pressure to refuse loans to countries for the production of foods that were seen to be competitive with products grown in the U.S. At the same time he was encouraged by moves in the other direction, to de-politicize development efforts by separating them from military goals.[20]

Soon there was solid evidence for increased government support for LWR development efforts. In September, 1979, Executive Director Confer announced that Lutheran World Relief had been awarded a one-million-dollar matching grant from the U.S. Agency for International Development. In addition, terms of the agreement provided for possible grants of an additional two million in the next two years.

Confer reported that LWR was receiving more and better project proposals than ever before, and that this grant would permit important expansion of the agency's services. He estimated that as many as 75 new projects could be funded from the grants during the next three years, including work in agricultural development, community health, staff training for overseas counterpart agencies, and project evaluation.[21]

Mutual Emphasis on Evaluation

Government agencies were giving increased attention to evaluation of projects, a concern that coincided with LWR's own thinking. Robert Busche, after a three-month visit to Central and South America in

1978, had led in a review of programs and relationships that stimulated a reassessment of LWR's entire approach to Latin America.

Busche called attention to competition between agencies in the north for "good places to enter work," and the striving by agencies in the south to compile records of achievement in order to attract more funds. He had concluded that a key stumbling block had been the difficulty in improving the "participatory process," involving local churches, communities, and individuals in the development effort. There was always a fear that local agencies, instead of using grants to move toward self-sufficiency, might become overly dependent on outside assistance.

A preliminary assessment indicated that some of LWR's objectives in Latin America had been more fully achieved than others. For example, the goal to "stimulate programs designed to enhance the role of women in society," needed additional strengthening, although work was being undertaken locally through mothers' clubs, nutrition centers, sewing centers, and community garden programs.[22]

It was obvious that more thorough evaluation should involve specialists from both inside and outside Latin America. Fortunately, LWR's partner agencies, DIACONIA in Brazil and DIACONIA in Chile, were eager to participate. In 1978 DIACONIA/Brazil had been in existence for 10 years and was currently active in more than 800 communities, requiring extensive travel by 15 local staff members.[23] Although only limited evaluation had been possible, word concerning effectiveness of some of the projects had stimulated interest from other communities in training programs. Decisions would have to be made concerning possible extension of LWR work, not only in Brazil and Chile, but in Peru and Bolivia. The appointment of Hans Hoyer to become LWR's first field-based regional consultant, reported in the previous chapter, was due partly to this move toward more thorough evaluation.

Moving toward the eighties, then, Lutheran World Relief was poised to expand its work, but saw the need to take a close look at what was being accomplished and what was being proposed. This would be a major task for new leadership.

THE HORN OF AFRICA—refugees make a home. In Somalia, Sudan, Ethiopia, and Eritrea, the region knows progress (p. 166) as well as setbacks (p. 168).

"JESUS IS HOMELESS," says Mother Teresa of Calcutta, thanking LWR's Gene Thiemann for years' worth of quilts and blankets (p. 141).

"THE BLANKET MAN," Bill Genszler (right), inspired Lutherans in Wisconsin and Upper Michigan to help others through LWR for 42 years (pp. 109, 110).

DIRECTOR NORMAN BARTH holds 1986 U.S. presidential award to LWR for "vision, initiative and leadership" in the fight against hunger (p.166).

THE SECURITY TO CONTINUE helping others means encouraging awareness and generosity as well as ongoing Christian stewardship.

WANKAMA, NIGER, a village just south of the Sahara. LWR quilts reach distant arms via local partners, in this case Caritas.

"IF WE WANT PEACE, we have to defend the accords." Aid and advocacy helped bring El Salvadorian communities into the 1990s.

WARS AND OCCUPATION hobble development in the Middle East. A West Bank workshop offers youth a trade, but a future depends upon peace.

9

Fine-tuning the Management Instrument

From its earliest years, Lutheran World Relief had retained essentially the same leadership, as noted in chapter 7. During the eighties there were to be significant changes. When Paul Empie died in late 1979, Robert Marshall was elected to replace him as president. In 1978 Marshall had decided not to be a candidate for a third term as president of the Lutheran Church in America and moved onto the staff of Lutheran World Ministries, then accepted a position on the faculty of Lutheran Theological Southern Seminary. In 1981 Bernard Confer retired and Norman Barth was elected to succeed him. In 1980 Ove Nielsen had retired after 26 years as Confer's assistant. One other pioneer, Edwin A. Nerger, continued as a director until 1984, having been involved with LWR for 30 years, many of them as secretary of the board.

To many people Confer had personified Lutheran World Relief, administering the agency like an artist playing an instrument. He was known and respected by officials of the many cooperating agencies. He kept in touch with LWR staff members throughout the world and made personal visits to areas where they were at work. He cultivated the support of church leaders and was sensitive to the convictions of Lutheran constituents. On occasion he struggled to make decisions he knew would be unpopular with some contributors, as when LWR engaged in services to Vietnamese as former enemies. Commenting on his dilemma at that time, he explained, "Whenever we hit something like this in LWR we have to ask ourselves which is more important, the full acceptance of our people or doing what we believe to be right according to Lutheran theology and biblical teaching." He added, "We have to take both into account." [1]

At Confer's death in 1988 Robert Marshall paid tribute to him as "a living epistle who always communicated to us Christ's concern for persons in need." Marshall pointed to Confer's insistence on the LWR principle of helping all persons in need regardless of their faith, and his emphasis on development and self-determination for the poor and oppressed. Quoting the words of the Apostle Paul, "It is no longer I who live, but Christ who lives in me," Marshall said, "I saw that in Bernie Confer." [2]

Confer and Ove Nielsen had operated as a productive partnership. Confer had little interest in writing extensive documents but Nielsen welcomed such assignments. Nielsen was an innovator who was inclined to make decisions quickly; Confer was the administrator who studied all proposals carefully before approving actions. According to Nielsen, Confer "had an uncanny ability to live with a workload and postpone decisions until he was ready to make them.... He had an unusual ability to hear things and sort them out and then come back with a kind of response that sometimes nearly floored us with the rationality...." [3] Confer obviously recognized Nielsen's innovative capacities. In a letter sent to Nielsen who was traveling in Korea at the time, Confer wrote, "Life goes on rather quietly here at the office. We miss the man who stirs things up!" [4]

Confer had worked closely with presidents Fry, Empie, and briefly with Marshall. The new team of Marshall and Barth was in a strategic position to take new initiatives. Marshall had been a director for ten years and was sensitive to LWR tradition but also recognized that changed conditions could create a need for adjustments in management style. He combined a deep commitment to LWR objectives with an incisive mind that could summarize complex issues and facilitate thoughtful deliberation.

Norman Barth brought a new dimension to the LWR staff. He had spent nearly 25 years as a career diplomat with the U.S. foreign service, occupying seven posts in three European and two African countries. His experience helped him, as well as other staff members, to relate wisely to government officials. He and Marshall were well qualified to guide Lutheran World Relief in assessing accomplishments and establishing directions for the future.

Realignment of Constituents

Immediately at the beginning of their administration, the new leaders had to anticipate changes in their constituency. Three of the four participating church bodies, The American Lutheran Church, the Lutheran Church in America, and the Association of Evangelical Lutheran Churches, were moving toward formation of one new church. Two coordinating agencies, the Lutheran Council in the U.S.A. and Lutheran World Ministries, would no longer exist. By 1988 The Lutheran Church—Missouri Synod and the new body, to be called the Evangelical Lutheran Church in America, would be the only two churches to be officially represented in governance and support of

Lutheran World Relief. The dream of a single church to represent nearly all Lutherans in the U.S. was not to be fulfilled at this time, but could there be common expression of faith in service to others? How would LWR be affected?

Soon after taking office, Barth met with the presidents of all four churches still in existence: Ralph Bohlmann of LCMS, David Preus of ALC, William Kohn of AELC, and James Crumley of LCA. Happily, there was general agreement that the realignment should cause no disruption in the operation of Lutheran World Relief.[5] All of these four executives, along with their predecessors and successors, were continually supportive of LWR. Three of the four served as LWR directors at one time or another and the fourth, David Preus, made on-site visits to development operations and used his many speaking opportunities to encourage support for LWR.

At the time of Lutheran World Relief's fortieth anniversary in 1985 the heads of all four church bodies, Bohlmann, Preus, Crumley, and Will L. Herzfeld, then president of the Association of Evangelical Lutheran Churches, issued statements of celebration. Ralph Bohlmann emphasized that LWR "has not only served in helping to meet the physical and spiritual needs which are so evident in our world. It has also provided an avenue for those whom God has blessed so bountifully for serving others as they share the blessings which have been given to them." [6]

Since the new ELCA would be twice as large as LCMS, there was a question as to how the two bodies should be represented on the board. The matter was resolved by allocating seven positions to the ELCA and four to LCMS, with the provision that a two-thirds vote would be required for action on basic policy matters and for the election of an executive director. Thus LCMS, although outnumbered in membership, could not be dominated in crucial issues.

The Wisconsin Evangelical Lutheran Synod, although invited into full membership, did not elect to enter officially into the new relationship but did continue to send observers to board meetings and to contribute to LWR projects. On at least one occasion LWR representatives participated in a study retreat with WELS staff members.

Lutheran World Relief also continued its relationships with other nongovernmental agencies. LWR participated actively in InterAction, an organization that succeeded the old American Council of Voluntary Agencies for Foreign Service, to which LWR had belonged since its earliest years. In 1987 LWR joined the InterFaith Hunger Appeal, facilitating cooperation among Protestant, Roman Catholic, and Jewish agencies. In a pluralistic society, there was wisdom and merit in working with other faiths to present the needs of the poor.

Assured of continuing support from the new ELCA and LCMS, LWR leaders could concentrate on how to achieve the greatest effectiveness in carrying out their increasingly complex tasks. Norman Barth concluded that a system appropriate for the limited objectives of post-World War II was not adequate for LWR's extensive commitments; the administrative instrument needed fine tuning. He decided to make some changes, and was encouraged by Robert Marshall who, while president of the Lutheran Church in America, had led in the adoption of a plan for that church's structure to clarify lines of responsibility while providing for extensive consultation at all levels.

Change in Governance

Between 1981 and 1988 the number of LWR development projects and responses to emergencies increased from 107 to nearly 300. Annual expenditures, which had hovered around $9 million dollars at the beginning of the decade, averaged $34 million between 1985 and 1989, and peaked at more than $90 million in 1990. Much of this increase came from U.S. funds for emergencies; of the $90 million in 1990 more than $80 million were provided by government sources.[7] In general, government funds accounted for 85% of LWR relief costs, but only 15% of development investments.

Traditionally, each project required approval by the board before it could be implemented. This became frustrating to both staff members and directors. Action was delayed and directors were confronted by proposals which they were unable to evaluate wisely within the time limits of meetings. Norman Barth asked, "Should these highly expert individuals spend their time looking at projects, adding up figures? Or should they be establishing policies which set the course of LWR's mission?" There was unanimous support for his proposal to establish clear policies within which the executive director and staff could make decisions about specific projects.[8]

The result placed responsibility on staff members who were most knowledgeable about specific situations and increased their credibility with partners. It was also encouraging to partner agencies by reducing the time required for responses to their proposals. Eventually it made possible a reduction in the number and expense of board meetings.

For staff guidance the provisions in the strategy document adopted in 1975 and reported in chapter 8 were still applicable. In 1979 and 1980 criteria for entering into new geographic areas were identified:

1. The receptivity of the people and government of an area.
2. The extent of need by the poorest majority.
3. Involvement of other agencies, and prospects for cooperation rather than duplication.
4. Availability of qualified personnel.
5. Prospects for adequate resources to see the program through to completion.

The comparative value of large and small projects was also studied, plus the potential effects of bilateral and multilateral funding.[9]

Under the new administration all of the earlier documents were examined, sharpened, and expanded into a policy statement adopted in 1985, amended in 1991, and currently under review. The statement of LWR's purpose reads, "to act on behalf of Lutherans in the U.S.A. to support the poor and oppressed of less-developed countries in their efforts to meet basic human needs and to participate with dignity and equity in the life of their communities; and to alleviate human suffering resulting from natural disaster, war, social conflict or poverty." Nondiscrimination and purposeful cooperation are identified as operational principles.

The executive is given a number of directives to follow before initiating a food aid program. Among them, he or she is now expected to ascertain the proportion of the emergency, the availability of aid from all sources, and the likely conditions of distribution. The most difficult requirement with which to comply is the one "to ensure that the food aid itself and/or the manner in which it is distributed will be unlikely to produce negative effects of a kind which would offset the benefits (e.g., serious depression of regional food prices, disincentive to production, sale of donated food)."

Development is newly defined as "the process by which people collectively address and seek to mitigate the causes and consequences of poverty, hunger, sickness, ignorance and injustice. Its aim is to achieve more fully the God-given human potential of all community members, creating more caring and just communities in which all members have access to means for meeting their basic human needs for food, shelter, clothing, employment, health care, and human development."

The people with whom development is to be carried on, previously identified as the "poorest of the poor," or the "poor majority," are now described by the term, "marginal communities." They are "people in localities or countries who are unable, de facto, to participate beneficially in the dominant economic, social, and political systems. Living at the margin of human existence, they are unable to influence or change the systems which effectively thwart their efforts to meet their basic human needs. Such communities are marked by widespread poverty, hunger, malnutrition, illness, unemployment, low life expectancy, high infant mortality, lack of educational opportunity, or other means of improving their condition."

Guidelines for allocating resources for development assistance are essentially the same as earlier ones previously cited, with a few additions. Provision is to be made for participation by women, and family planning activities are to be considered "in the context of an integrated program of community health and development, and in a way that is consistent with the policies of supporting church bodies."

The executive director is also urged to provide support for programs which "provide a reconciling and healing ministry in situations where the aspirations of the poor and oppressed in less developed countries are frustrated by social conflict and war."

The policy statement also recognizes the need for development education among constituents, and for offering advice on public policy. Such advice from LWR is to be limited "to areas within its experience and competence and related to its mission." Efforts by ecumenical partners within the developing nations to engage in consciousness-raising and advocacy on behalf of the poor are to be supported. Reflecting the emerging emphasis on the importance of systemic change, LWR is to support the work of multilateral organizations "which address the causes of poverty and suffering through social and economic changes, seeking reconciliation and healing rather than division and strife."

Responsibilities of the board are now concentrated on providing linkage to the supporting churches, reviewing and enunciating policies, and assuring executive performance by monitoring compliance with policies. Guidelines are provided for assuring integrity in financial and personnel management. All in all, the policy now gives the executive and staff significant operating authority, while expecting the board to provide for clear guidance and review.[10]

To insure compliance with the revised policies, each department began establishing annual goals, then reporting on accomplishments or failures, documented by specific information concerning projects.

To carry on sharply increased services in this manner required attention to staffing both at home and abroad.

Central Program Staffing for the Future

Robert Busche continued as assistant executive director in charge of LWR's Central and South America programs until, in 1984, he became senior advisor to the executive director for policy and development programs, continuing in that capacity until his retirement in 1989. Busche was a strong advocate for strengthened program evaluation and, according to Barth, was responsible for LWR's "think pieces." [11]

To replace Ove Nielsen, Neil Brenden served until 1985 as assistant, then associate executive director. He had worked on behalf of LWR in Vietnam and Nigeria, in addition to serving other agencies in the U.S. and abroad.[12] From the New York offices he first directed programs for east Africa and Asia, then concentrated on Asia and the Middle East.

There were frequent shifts in direction of programs for Africa and Latin America. After assisting Brenden for two years, Ellen Jorgenson agreed to oversee programs in Niger and Togo for three years. Robert Cottingham as director and James Noss as assistant, both with mission experience in Africa, devoted three years each to coordinating relief and development programs for that continent. Frank Conlon was brought from service in Africa to become director in 1987. He was assisted for two years by Lisa Henry and for a short time by Jeff Whisenant, who was also assistant to the executive director and who, in 1993, became program director for Latin America. He had been preceded in that role by Kenneth Brown, Jr., and Thomas Edwards, who served from 1986 until 1990, when he became LWR's Andean representative. At that time Kathryn Wolford came from service in Latin America to New York to direct that program until being elected as executive director in 1993.

Interpretation

The end of the Lutheran Council in the U.S.A. meant also the end of its News Bureau and other promotional services provided LWR. The

ELCA World Hunger program helped to fill that gap, and LCMS World Relief continued its informational services. *Sharing*, the bimonthly newsletter of LCMS, has been especially effective. But Lutheran World Relief also needed to expand its own interpretative efforts. Journalists from member churches were assisted in visiting overseas programs and reporting on them. New printed materials, films, and filmstrips were produced each year. Videogames and T-shirts were produced for youth gatherings. Videotapes received special attention. In 1988, for example, the video, "Flying Quilts," demonstrated how quilts and other items prepared by women's groups fly "in spirit" to places like Tanzania. The LWR venture in arid regions of Africa was portrayed vividly in the film, *When the Harvest Comes*.

Some supporters of LWR periodically advocate "going public," including the use of mass media to solicit gifts from persons having no connection with Lutheranism. Aside from concern as to what effect this might have on the basic orientation of LWR, any such attempt also confronts the reality that public media have become so commercially oriented that their use by humanitarian agencies often consumes most of the income raised. LWR has offered public service announcements to television stations, including one featuring an animated character, "World Turtle," who emphasizes that development is not a quick fix by saying, "Slow and steady wins the race." [13] No appreciable amount of income has resulted, but any public reference to LWR probably strengthens Lutheran viewers in their identification with the agency. Staff members continue to explore opportunities for making more of a public impact.

In 1987 Gene Thiemann, after more than a decade as director of interpretation, moved to program director for Asia and the Middle East. William Dingler then became director of interpretation and continued in the position until his retirement in 1993. Jonathan Frerichs took over as director for communication in 1994.

Parish Projects

Interpretation of LWR's services was aided immensely by the involvement of thousands of church members in the creation and collection of items needed in the field. Quilters have always been among LWR's most loyal supporters. The 1982 spring appeal used the

theme, "Give a quilt; be a comforter." [14] Quilts displayed in congregations, conventions, and assemblies have focused the attention of
thousands on the work of Lutheran World Relief. In 1994 more than
1800 quilting groups, representing 24,000 participants, were recognized
with certificates for their devoted service. Staff members were certain
that hundreds of other groups were not yet identified.[15]

While needs have varied among different types of clothing, quilts
have remained valuable, along with school, health, and sewing kits,
layettes, and soap. For the last ten years, the value of these items
collected and distributed by LWR has averaged more than five million
dollars annually. In a typical year, 1986, the shipments included
228,371 quilts or blankets, more than 300,000 pounds of soap, 60,744
health kits, 22,302 school kits, 21,825 sewing kits, and 39,960
layettes.[16]

Edna Wagschal had supervised these efforts as secretary for
special projects for 14 years when she retired in 1989. Anna Belle
Thiemann succeeded her.

At Norman Barth's instigation, LWR in the eighties entered into
another relationship with constituents, study tours to visit project areas.
Gene Thiemann led the first group of 12 individuals to Tanzania and
Kenya in 1985 and Edna Wagschal led a similar two-week tour to
Senegal, Mauritania, Niger, and Togo in 1986. Subsequent tours have
gone regularly to other areas.[17]

Direct exposure to the work in progress gives participants a greater
appreciation for LWR's services than can be conveyed through any
intermediary. In some places the visitors, representing a tie with
otherwise unknown and distant partners, are hugged by appreciative
local citizens. Once, when visitors who were also veteran quilt-makers,
watched quilts being distributed, an observer was inspired by what he
saw in the faces of both the refugee recipients and the quilters.[18] As
a result of a similar visit to a women's lacemaking project stimulated
by LWR in India, at least two craft shops in the U.S. are handling
embroidered baptismal napkins and bookmarks made there. The local
women were already marketing their lace as far away as Belgium,
generating their own income. The opening of an American market for
their wares strengthened ties with the agency that had helped them to
get started. One of the American visitors commented concerning the
baptismal napkins, "How appropriate that these napkins, which bring
hope for a new life to those who make them, are used when a new life

in Christ comes to His little ones." [19] Many participants in the tours take advantage of extensive speaking opportunities when they return to their home communities.

Special Gifts

From the beginning Lutheran World Relief had received in the mail some direct contributions from individuals. By the eighties as many as 5,000 people were sending such unsolicited gifts annually to the New York office, but executives faced a dilemma. LWR was prohibited from soliciting contributions directly from congregations or individual members. It was appropriate, however, to send letters of appreciation for gifts, and even this limited contact tended to encourage additional giving. LWR had a well-deserved reputation for exercising the best of stewardship in the use of funds and, especially when a catastrophe abroad received extensive media coverage, thoughtful persons were motivated to send a contribution directly to an agency they trusted.

Staff and board members recognized two other factors that caused them to reconsider their policy. Many members of Lutheran congregations were known to contribute substantially to agencies outside their church, and LWR might tap into this resource without affecting congregational support. It was also true that there were thousands of nominal Lutherans who had no contact with churches but might welcome the opportunity to participate financially in LWR's efforts. After receiving approval from officials of the member church bodies, the board in 1991 authorized a modest expansion of the special gifts program. Staff was encouraged to explore supplemental fund-raising activities among individuals who had already contributed directly to LWR. Direct mailings were begun four times a year, with clear references to specific ventures of LWR but only low-key references to funding. Initial results have been encouraging. Contributions of this kind have increased from less than $700,000 per year to more than $1,000,000. An important function of the letters is to educate individuals concerning LWR's extensive services.[20]

A succession of staff members had responsibility for maintaining these contacts—Alice Smith, Betty Nute, Connie David, and Linda Freudenberg, before June Braun became secretary for special gifts in 1985.

In the nineties LWR also began receiving income from a new source through membership in the International Service Agencies.

Payroll deductions from church members working at federal, state, and local government levels made it possible for Barth to report, in September, 1993, that the amount channeled to LWR from this fund had risen from zero to $500,000 in three years.[21]

Office on Development Policy

In Washington Carol Capps in 1979 became an associate with Larry Minear as representative for what was soon known as the Office on Development Policy. Cheryl Morden became an assistant in 1985 and associate in 1991, when Minear moved to other ventures and Capps became director.

Washington staff members established and maintained ties between LWR and government officials. They shared with administrators and members of Congress overseas experiences that could shed light on policies and legislation. They prodded authorities to act more speedily in emergencies. They called attention to the vulnerability of colleagues providing humanitarian aid in repressive situations, as in Central America. They provided background material for Norman Barth and Robert Marshall to use in correspondence and in testimony before government committees. Much of their work consisted of participating in the ongoing debate over periodic revisions in U.S. foreign aid programs. A continuing frustration was the question as to how constituents in the supporting churches could become more involved in convincing the Congress that many Americans do have humanitarian concerns.

One goal that remained constant through the years was to influence legislation to increase funding for humanitarian aid. With the decline in cold war tensions, reduction in military expenditures appeared to be a reasonable source of dollars. Modest improvements were made in grants for Africa, especially, but during the eighties security assistance continued to receive nearly two-thirds of U.S. foreign aid; resources for humanitarian aid represented only one-quarter of one percent of U.S. Gross National Product, placing the U.S. at the bottom of the list of 17 Western donor nations in terms of that category.[22] LWR took the position that humanitarian assistance was a greater factor in national security than financial outlays for warfare and destruction. One related concern was to oppose the existing practice of labeling as "humanitarian" the supplies and goods being sent to combat forces in Nicaragua. It was not until 1992 that an appropriations bill reduced military and security assistance by more than a billion dollars and shifted resources to humanitarian and development assistance.[23]

Staff members of the Office on Development Policy had been urging Congress and administrators to give more attention to development, to engage in consultation with the people in need, to give priority to small farmers, and to demonstrate special concern for women who, in many countries, were suffering from the greatest neglect. In 1989 funding was increased for programs assisting women from both the U.S. Agency for International Development and two United Nations agencies. The ODP provided leadership in discussions with staff from the World Bank, International Monetary Fund, and U.S. Treasury Department about the impact of debt and "structural adjustment" on the poor. Actions by those agencies often appeared to be shoring up the wealthy of countries without improving the lot of the poor.[24]

The Office on Development Policy has always collaborated with many other agencies here and abroad, consulting regularly in research and advocacy. Staff members have stressed the importance of retaining the private and voluntary nature of agencies like LWR. They have also spearheaded conferences involving overseas governments and voluntary agencies, along with UN representatives, designed to encourage grass-roots participation in all forms of development.[25]

ODP's familiarity with government policies has had some value for LWR program personnel in dealing with agencies providing financial support for LWR projects. Grants from the Agency for International Development have been substantial, although declining. From $3 million for three years in 1979, the matching grant for a similar period in 1983 was $2.3 million. Then in 1985 the funding for a five-year period was $2.5 million. Along the way, LWR officials acquired enough reservations about the relationship to make them delay applying for additional AID grants. The paperwork had become excessive, but there were more serious concerns. AID appeared to be placing increasing restraints on the management of programs and using partners to carry out AID's own purposes, not always in accord with LWR emphases. There was hope, however, that policy changes could remedy the situation.[26]

Administration of Resources

While the National Lutheran Council and, later, the Lutheran Council in the U.S.A. were operating, they were able to provide some finance and personnel services for Lutheran World Relief. With that option closing in the eighties and needs expanding, administrative changes became necessary. Joseph Sprunger, with experience in India and Vietnam, began serving as director for grant relations in 1980, but his assignments were soon expanded and in 1984 he became director for finance and administration, with oversight responsibilities extending to the broad range of material and human resources. Sprunger also counseled periodically with overseas partners concerning problems in administration. Sheila Kammerer continued as program finance manager until 1985, when she was replaced by Candy Eng, who became comptroller in 1987. In that capacity she oversees day-to-day financial matters, assisted by Arlene DeAbreu as accounting supervisor. In 1985, also, Ann Fries was employed as manager for human resources. Walter A. Jensen, who for many years supervised LWR financial services while an executive with NLC and LCUSA, has remained as the official LWR treasurer.[27]

One key position on the LWR staff is still occupied by a veteran, Kenneth Killen. In service with LWR since 1957 and in charge of shipping for more than a decade when the eighties began, Killen has had various titles including the most descriptive, director for material resources. Since 1970 he has been ably assisted by Roland Fritchman.

Killen's first mentor, Carl Lorey, indoctrinated him in a rigid principle of financial stewardship. When Killen asked approval for the expenditure of $1.50 to purchase an "in-box" for his papers, Lorey replied, "Do you know how many children we can feed for $1.50?" For six months Killen got along without his in-box; he could not be annoyed with Lorey because of the man's deep commitment. Killen himself became deeply dedicated to his work, observing, "When you see a mother picking through garbage to give food to her children, then you are face to face with poverty." But through the years he developed a more discriminating sense of economy. Once, for example, a ship carrying food for starving people in the Sudan sailed before its official papers could be secured. When the documents finally reached Killen just before the ship was to reach port, he took action. Knowing that the ship could not be unloaded without the papers, he did not hesitate to invest in an airline ticket enabling him to fly abroad to deliver them.[28]

As Killen supervised the shipping of material items, he had to adapt to changing needs in the use of warehouses. LWR's first contract, in 1945, was with Easton Processing and Storage Company of Easton, Pennsylvania, to receive, sort, and package the clothing, shoes, and blankets for shipping primarily to Germany. With expansion of service to other countries, LWR contracted in 1951 with the Church of the Brethren for use of their facilities in New Windsor, Maryland, and Nappanee, Indiana. To feed into the processing centers at Easton and New Windsor, additional facilities were made available in Seattle, Minneapolis, Los Angeles, and San Francisco. Later, centers were operated in San Antonio and Chicago. The Church of the Brethren also expanded their warehousing to St. Louis, Houston, Denver, Pasadena, Modesto, and Vancouver. With LWR's increasing concentration on work in tropical climates where heavy clothing was no longer needed, it was unnecessary to maintain as many warehouses, so the number was first reduced to six between 1970 and 1973, then in 1985 to two, in New Windsor and Minneapolis, where operation continues.[29]

Offices Overseas

The most obvious change in LWR operations in the eighties was the establishment of additional overseas offices, some of them for individual countries, others for larger geographical areas. On the surface this could be interpreted as a departure from the traditional emphasis on encouraging local responsibility, but it was actually intended to move in that direction. The offices were not expected to design or implement projects but to explore local needs and opportunities. Their immediate purpose was to identify local agencies with whom to establish working relationships. Where no such agencies existed, work often could be undertaken with persons who could eventually establish the kind of organization needed to become a partner. This was never necessary in India or the Philippines, where there was no lack of potential partners.

In some cases, especially in country offices, plans could be made at the beginning for their dissolution within a specific period of time. Elsewhere, especially in regional offices, it seemed desirable to maintain a presence to share experiences from elsewhere and to provide an opportunity for continuing consultation. Representatives on the scene could be helpful also in arranging for visits by board members and staff from the New York office, and by helping to interpret the work to constituents in the home churches.

Such active partnership does appear to run counter to the position of some development theorists who favor a policy of allocating funds almost exclusively to "block grants," contributions made available to overseas agencies for use in whatever way is desired by them. Advocates of country and regional offices counter that position by maintaining that LWR has much more than money to contribute to partnerships. Consultation does not imply domination. LWR staff members, prompted by Robert Busche, always recognized the value of allowing others to learn from their own mistakes. But active partnership can contribute to learning by all participants. Peruvian Pedro Veliz has spoken appreciatively about the mutual respect generated in those consultative relationships; he values the "dose of constructive criticism that can be stimulated by questions." [30]

Before 1980 there had been a number of country offices, some of them to facilitate short-term emergency efforts, but the only regional one was in the Andes, established in 1979 in Lima to serve Peru, Bolivia, Ecuador, and Chile. Its first director was Hans Hoyer, who had previous, extensive experience in Latin America. He served there until moving to East Africa in 1986, when Jerry Aaker replaced him. Aaker had served in Vietnam, Peru, and Nicaragua, and has provided a good description of the Andean "experiment" in his book, *Partners with the Poor*.[31] At his departure in 1991 Thomas Edwards left his New York post as director for Latin America to become the Andean regional representative; in 1994 Pedro Veliz replaced him. In 1987 the office had been relocated for security reasons in Quito, Ecuador, but in 1994 it was moved back to Lima.

A country office begun in the midseventies that evolved into a regional program exemplifies what was intended by this organizational approach. In the West African country of Niger LWR engaged in the familiar response to drought-related famine. When it became obvious that the shortage of food was related to more than temporary conditions, a series of representatives began assisting in attempts to improve the water supply and increase food production. At this time no local voluntary agencies were allowed by the government to operate in Niger, so overseas presence was essential. Dry season gardening became productive and was strengthened by efforts in forestry, health, literacy and community development. Similar efforts were undertaken in Togo, in cooperation with the counterpart agency, SOTOPRODER, the Togolese Association for the Promotion of Rural Development.

In 1983 Frank J. Conlon, Jr., became country director in Niger. He was familiar with the LWR venture because he had been in Niger as a Peace Corps volunteer in the seventies. Developments in Niger were progressing so steadily that more projects were being undertaken there than in the Asian and Latin American regions combined. This allocation could be supported by the fact that African countries had been making less progress against food scarcity than on the other continents. Missing ingredients in the local enterprises, such as wells, seeds, fertilizers and tools, were being loaned with reimbursement coming to the local communities.

Conlon began almost immediately to explore possibilities for sharing LWR's experiences with nearby countries facing similar problems. He realized that more on-site staff would be needed for starting such an undertaking, and in 1986 Lutheran World Relief established additional offices in Mali, Burkina Faso, and Senegal. In Niger Conlon headed a staff of twenty, four of whom were Americans, but the new offices had only one westerner each and all were given only three to five years to accomplish the task of identifying or encouraging the establishment of local agencies to carry on future operations. This was accomplished by 1990. Norman Barth pointed out to the LWR directors that the governments of all of the countries involved in the expanded program had expressed their appreciation for the LWR approach, which he described as "evolving a program of assistance that works to empower people at the grass roots to identify basic problems and work toward sustainable solutions."[32] In some of the countries, especially Niger, individual government employees, such as agricultural agents, became most active in cooperating with LWR.

Conlon was brought to New York in 1987, from where he could oversee the West African work for as long as the four country offices, including the one in Niger, existed. With the closing of the three temporary ones it became important to have a regional director on the scene and, in 1990, John Soloninka, who had been a missionary in Senegal, was appointed to that post, based in Niamey, Niger. There were many spinoffs from LWR projects being undertaken in the countries where offices had been closed, and there was need for consultation to be made available.

Meanwhile, in 1983, a regional office had been opened in Nairobi, Kenya, to serve East Africa, where famine was regularly affecting many countries. The location in Nairobi facilitated agency cooperation by being the base also for area offices of Church World Service, Catholic Relief Services, and World Service of the Lutheran World Federation. Thomas L. Roach, a former Peace Corps and CARE official, was named the first director, with responsibilities extending to the Sudan, where a country office also operated for several critical years, in addition to Ethiopia, Somalia, Tanzania, Uganda, Burundi, and Rwanda. Hans Hoyer came from the Andes to become director in 1986 and Sigurd Hanson followed him in 1989.[33]

Volunteer Program

One promising program to recruit personnel for overseas assignments was undertaken in the eighties but proved to be more costly than anticipated and was discontinued. In the summer of 1982 LWR joined with Lutheran World Ministries, Canadian Lutheran World Relief, and National Lutheran Campus Ministry to arrange for 22 students and three staff members to live for six weeks in Zimbabwe or Tanzania, working together with residents of those countries in combating hunger and meeting the challenges of nation-building. The plan called next for 10 college-aged volunteers with appropriate skills to be sent annually for two-year assignments in overseas development projects. They were to receive room and board, medical insurance, and a small monthly stipend.

In 1983 five volunteers began participating in the program. One served as an assistant in LWR's Andean regional office in Lima, Peru. Three became teachers of mathematics and English at a school in Tanzania, and the fifth served as technician and trainer of other technicians in Tanzania.

The cross-cultural experience was valuable for participants, and they contributed to the communities they served. A number of them became full-time development workers, including Jeff Whisenant, currently LWR's program director for Latin America. But expenses doubled projections and it became obvious that more staff time was needed to train and stay in consultation with the volunteers. Officials reluctantly terminated the program, hoping to find a way to resume it at a later date.[34] Such attention to cost-effectiveness had become normal operating procedure; all projects were subject to careful evaluation.

Are We Gaining or Losing Ground?

When Lutheran World Relief began its ministry, there was no need for a research project to measure its accomplishments. Thousands of people had been rescued from starvation. Hope was restored in cities and villages. Germany, the focus of most of the original LWR efforts, regained its vitality despite its political division.

By the eighties, LWR was attempting to direct its efforts toward more than immediate relief. The original function of dealing with disasters, however, demanded continuing attention. There were understandable regrets that so much money and staff time had to be channeled to deal with temporary crises rather than long-term development. But there was no thought of discontinuing relief. Mother Teresa of Calcutta provided a reminder of the value of immediate help when Gene Thiemann visited her on behalf of LWR. She was grateful for all of the quilts sent by LWR for her ministry, and volunteered that she was aware of the importance of teaching people to fish rather than simply giving them fish to eat, but she insisted, "God has called me to give the fish!" Asked what kept her going in her grueling schedule she answered, "Jesus is the bread of life, and he has said that unless you eat you cannot live. And Jesus has said that he's the hungry one, he's the naked one, he's the homeless one." [1]

In 1992, when Norman Barth looked back on 11 years as LWR director, he recalled especially certain major disasters: 1984-85, African famine; 1987, recurrence of Ethiopian drought; 1988, Armenian earthquake; 1990, Liberian civil war; and 1991, Kurdish crisis. Then in 1992 there were crises in the former Yugoslavia, Somalia, southern Sudan, Lebanon, and eastern and southern Africa. [2] In addition to all of these, each year in parts of Africa, Asia, and Latin America there were less publicized cyclones, earthquakes, epidemics, droughts and floods, and flights of refugees from military and political conflicts. The combination was so overwhelming that it was natural to wonder, at times, how much was being achieved by relief efforts.

Distinctive Contributions

As an agency closely related to churches throughout the world, Lutheran World Relief has functioned as an early warning system concerning impending tragedies such as famines. LWR has also been able to react more quickly than government agencies.

The famine in the "Horn of Africa," comprising Ethiopia, Somalia, and the Sudan, became the focus of global relief efforts in late 1984 after a film clip from the British Broadcasting Corporation was shown on American television. But LWR had been one of the first agencies to recognize the magnitude of that drought. An airlift into Somalia had been supported already in 1982 and in 1983 LWR tried to alert the churches to what was even then a major catastrophe in Ethiopia. World Hunger coordinators of supporting churches distributed packets on the plight of Africa to Lutheran pastors. At the same time LWR began devoting millions of dollars to the African emergency.[3] Robert Marshall saw this as especially appropriate for such an agency. He explained, "It should be expected when there is suffering in far-off places that Christians should respond first. Before the news media and governments pay attention, usually church agencies are at work. When the others join in, these agencies have laid the groundwork to get the job done." [4]

Service to Ethiopia in the midst of a civil war involved a venture in peacemaking that will be given special attention in chapter 11, but the relief effort by itself was impressive. LWR joined in a partnership which included other Lutherans, Roman Catholics, and the Ethiopian Orthodox Church in an effort described in full by Richard W. Solberg in his book, *Miracle in Ethiopia*.[5] Enormous quantities of food, medicine, clothing, and quilts, plus seed and tools were supplied to people in areas under central government control.

Even in the midst of a catastrophe, LWR and partner agencies were reminded of their accountability. Was the food actually getting to the hungry? Critics questioned whether relief agencies could make responsible use of the huge sums given them. Operating among people engaged in a civil war did create special risks. The military could make equitable distribution difficult. The combatants, including some who were only children, could be hungry themselves, or could insist on providing for their own families. Rumors could arise from misunderstandings. In Ethiopia, for example, the burlap bags in which grain was transported were themselves a valuable commodity. Long after the grain had been eaten, it was not unusual for the bags to be sold several times. A bag observed for sale in a marketplace could contain wood, salt, or fertilizer, instead of donated food.

But LWR was taking every possible precaution. Norman Barth replied to those who questioned what was happening:

> Let me suggest to these critics that they leave their offices...and come with me or any member of my staff and see not only the crushing human need, but the responsible way in which the resources are being distributed. Let them see parents sitting on their haunches for hours in the hot African sun waiting for their names to be called from a list with their family size noted. Let them come with me as these people are given grain in exact measures sufficient for 30 days. Let them come with me as these people press their thumbs on the form acknowledging receipt of the food.[6]

By the end of 1986 a report from the U.S. Senate Judiciary Committee said that seven million lives had been saved in Ethiopia and cited the "incredible work and sacrifices of the international and voluntary agencies." [7]

Lutheran World Relief strengthened its own capability by enlisting a number of people to assist during the emergency. In New York John Tenhula, who had worked with the Sudan Council of Churches, Church World Service, and the United Nations High Commissioner for Refugees, was employed to deal with the U.S. Agency for International Development and monitor progress in the delivery of grain provided by that agency. To deal with complex logistics involved in the delivery of shipments to Port Sudan, LWR contracted for the services of Ian Christoplos, who had more than four years of experience as a port expediter in New Orleans. Two missionaries were seconded to expedite service in the Sudan and Ethiopia: Hector Ottemoeller, a "can-do type of individual" from LCMS, and Harlan Gilbertson, an agricultural specialist, from ALC.[8]

Meanwhile, Lutheran World Relief's capacity to lead in identifying and reacting to crises was achieving results on other continents. In 1983 the ocean current known as El Nino caused great wind and temperature shifts, leading to one of the most powerful weather disturbances in history. Cycles of drought and flooding endangered many nations, especially in Latin America. Lutheran World Relief was able to respond quickly because of its relationships with counterpart agencies. In Bolivia and Peru, for example, LWR authorized funding of more than a million dollars; the decision could be made with confidence because the Andean Regional Office headed by Hans Hoyer worked with 34 different groups to implement assistance programs.[9]

When Iraq invaded Kuwait in 1990, tens of thousands of Arabs and Asian nationals fled for the relative safety of Jordan, where camps were hastily set up. LWR acted immediately by airlifting 16,000 quilts and blankets for the refugees and by making cash grants to the Middle East Council of Churches for temporary shelter and emergency food. The allied bombardment of Baghdad brought a new flood of refugees and additional quilts were sent. When missile attacks and the threat of chemical warfare spread to Israel and the West Bank, LWR helped the Lutheran World Federation purchase emergency supplies for its Augusta Victoria Hospital in Jerusalem. With the cease-fire in February, 1991, came a new need to deal with the plight of hundreds of thousands of fleeing Iraqi Kurds and Shiites. LWR again sent quilts and blankets plus children's clothing.[10]

In 1993 LWR moved quickly to help victims of a devastating earthquake that struck a remote part of central India, killing some 20,000 people. Having worked in that area for more than two decades, LWR responded with a $200,000 grant for food, water, medical aid, and temporary shelter. The assistance was channeled through LWR's long-time partner, the Church's Auxiliary for Social Action. Among CASA's resources were quilts from LWR in storage for distribution.[11]

Beyond Survival

All who were involved in LWR services were eager to give more attention to rehabilitation rather than relief. Without neglecting emergency services, Lutheran World Relief in the eighties tried to build on those experiences for more lasting efforts toward self-sufficiency. Attempts were made, for example, to avoid gathering people in refugee camps. Norman Barth testified at a congressional hearing in 1987, "It is much better to keep farmers on their own lands so they can maintain their strength, their tools, furniture, and homes. It is much better to keep the pastoralists with their animals so they do not feel the pressure to sell them. This is a way to escape the horrors of feeding camps and the disruption of the fragile subsistence economies of the area." [12]

The practice of giving food for work came under renewed consideration. In some instances this approach appeared to fall short of dealing with the true needs of communities, featuring short-term rather than long-term effects. In other areas, however, especially where food shortages were most severe, the program still had value. In the eighties food shipments went only to Africa, where the need was greatest.[13]

Wherever possible, LWR assisted people in moving beyond mere survival. The hope that had been revived by overcoming hunger and devastation was applied to the drive toward a fulfilling life. In this process LWR could be a welcome partner partly because of the respect gained from "accompanying" rather than dominating the relief enterprise. Gilberto Aguirre, now executive director of CEPAD, the development agency for the Nicaraguan Council of Churches, summarized the origin of such a meaningful relationship. He said, "LWR came to us 'as we were' and lived with us. At that time, none of us had houses, water, toilets, due to the earthquake. LWR accompanied us, in the best sense of the word. Communication was fluid, direct. The LWR staff person respected our culture and our customs. That respect was decisive in making CEPAD what it is." [14]

Pursuing long-term goals meant establishing more discriminating benchmarks. In dealing with relief from disaster, there could be satisfaction in knowing that the victims were fed, clothed, and temporarily housed. When the emphasis shifted to sustainable development, there could be legitimate questions concerning what was actually being accomplished and whether it was worth the investment.

Some projects could justify their existence simply by observation but major programs would require systematic evaluation.

Missing Ingredients

Lutheran World Relief's determination to work *with* people and not simply *for* them required a careful analysis of the local situation. In all areas where service was contemplated, both human and material resources were available. The crucial question became, "What is missing?" Sometimes the answer was obvious, and might even be a single item. In many areas, especially in parts of Africa, the critical ingredient lacking was water. With available, potable water, the entire, living environment could be improved.

Chapter 7 includes description of an initiative in Niger that led in the seventies to the development of a system for creating workable wells using precast concrete rings. These replaced traditional wells that were lined only with dirt and tree branches, and usually collapsed. Expenses were only a tenth of the investment in a capital-intensive system used by some governmental and international agencies. LWR took advantage of this new resource by supporting, in a number of villages, projects involving gardening and agriculture, forestry, health, literacy, and community development. Many results were obvious, but in this case a more systematic study was also authorized. After several years and an investment of more than half a million dollars, a thorough evaluation of eight projects was undertaken in 1982. Under a contract with Virginia Polytechnic Institute and State University a forester and an anthropologist were employed to meet in Niger with villagers and government officials. To measure objectives, 24 guideline points were identified to be rated as low, medium, high, or no impact. They included such standards as "How well can activities become self-supporting?" and "Stimulate communities' own development?"

The survey indicated that the projects produced encouraging results. In fact, the experts concluded, "From an overall perspective, their solid and consistent accomplishments are among the most meaningful and effective of any of the development efforts in the entire country." Results included 325 new wells, 4,000 acres of irrigated gardens, 700 tons of vegetables, plus related outputs in road construction, buildings, live fencing, educational and health delivery systems, and enhanced local management ability. Approximately 13,000 people benefited through improved water supply and increased food production, at an average cost of $44 per person.[15]

Constructing hand-dug wells using precast concrete rings confronted one serious problem. The cost was still more than the average gardener was able to pay, requiring outside funding for the work to be extended to the poorest areas. Experimentation in the eighties led to the development of a system of hand-augered wells, using drills that could be built locally and casing that could be secured from the Ivory Coast. After the procedure had been refined, it was possible to install a well extending five meters below the water table, with a total depth of 10 to 12 meters, in less than a day. The cost of less than $20 per meter brought the wells within a figure that could be earned from their operation.[16]

Techniques developed in one location were often applied elsewhere. Hand-augered wells provided the stimulus to development in many areas. Another discovery served a similar purpose in Bangladesh, a country the size of Wisconsin but with more than 100 million people struggling to survive. Most exist on plots of land no larger than two acres. There a system was devised in the eighties to install a hollowed-out bamboo tube 10 to 40 feet into the ground. By connecting it with a simple treadle device, also made from bamboo, farmers could pump enough water for their small fields. Instead of one crop, they could harvest two or more yields of rice, wheat, or vegetables. Each month five workshops produced 2,000 bamboo pumps at a cost of $12 each.

With the bamboo equipment providing easy access to water, attention could be given to health habits, new crops, and compost. Next steps led to schools, cooperatives, functional literacy, and small-scale industry. A partnership utilizing a missing ingredient produced results that were both observable and measurable.[17]

Another significant discovery was made under Lutheran World Relief auspices in the eighties. In the Singida region of Tanzania, cooking oil, at $20 a liter, was an expensive and precious commodity. In partnership with the Evangelical Lutheran Church in Tanzania, LWR first found that sunflowers could be grown in Singida's arid climate. But the farmers had to sell their seeds, for processing into cooking oil, to a company using expensive, imported, diesel-powered presses. The farmers did not earn enough from the sale of their seeds to buy the resulting oil. So experimentation was undertaken to build a simple, hand-operated press that would not need to use expensive gasoline or diesel fuel. The resulting mechanism worked spectacularly well. It produced three liters per hour, nonstop because all residue was excreted automatically. This residue was an excellent source of protein for cows.

The price of cooking oil dropped to less than three dollars per liter and the low-cost, locally constructed machines allowed farmers to profit enough to provide for some of their family needs. Cooperatives were formed to offer training in the new industry and help in marketing. By 1991 the presses were being introduced in Zimbabwe, Lesotho, Kenya, and the Gambia, and adapted to use not only sunflower seeds but also other oil-yielding seeds and coconut.[18]

Not all missing ingredients were part of such extensive projects or had such widespread influence. Occasionally a small amount of outside resources could enable people to remove a purely local obstacle. In Ucayali, Peru, indigenous communities live in a remote jungle area, accessible only by water. To that area's Federation of Native Communities LWR in 1990 made a one-time grant of $2,000 to purchase an outboard motor for the community boat. This made possible transportation of crops and other products to the marketplace. Community representatives could travel to government offices to confer with officials there, and could meet with leaders of other similar groups. Sick people could be taken to clinics and health workers could commute. Native teachers could attend an annual convention. Passengers were charged a minimal amount to cover gasoline, maintenance, and payment to the boat pilots.   A relatively small contribution made a demonstrably large impact.[19]

Such results from providing missing ingredients were satisfying to observe, but Lutheran World Relief was involved in the eighties in efforts to bring long-term improvement to living conditions in widespread areas. To review strategy and be accountable to constituents, there was increasing need for reliable evidence of accomplishment in such programs.

Andean Regional Office Evaluation

LWR's first regional office had been established in the Andes in 1978 as a result of informal evaluation of the work already being carried on in the area. Since this decision reflected a new strategy, it was important to study its effectiveness as soon as possible. In 1982, therefore, a team of two consultants and an LWR representative undertook a thorough evaluation. Findings generally supported the decision; LWR enjoyed a high degree of regard from both indigenous and international agencies in the area. The team concluded that the office was supporting a significant number of highly participatory projects that were assisting low-income persons to meet their basic needs. LWR's capacity for promoting exchanges among agencies and communities was proving to be important. Concern was expressed that staff was overextended in its activity load, and the team suggested a number of remedial actions, including limitation in the number of countries served, hiring additional staff, and more careful planning. The office was urged to disseminate more widely information concerning the possible availability of "seed money" for small projects. Only limited impact was observed in the area of increasing management capabilities of local groups.

The evaluation team submitted a list of recommendations, including the development of a strategy paper, the preparation of an annual work plan for the entire staff, the adoption of an annual reporting system, and the establishment of an overall funding policy. The office was urged to work even more closely with other agencies involved in the same pursuits, rather than attempting to act independently.[20]

It was obvious that such evaluations could be helpful, and that they should be scheduled every few years. In 1987 another one was undertaken in the region, and its overall findings were again supportive. Knowing that LWR was attempting to apply the practice of "accompaniment" to all of its work, the experts observed that the Andean office was meeting perceived needs and was making a difference in the community. The report stated that LWR "has shown the centers that it is possible for a foreign donor agency to behave in a way which is more acceptable to both parties." It was clear that LWR was reacting with sensitivity to a widespread perception that donor agencies often behaved in an imperialist fashion. There was even a concern, however, that the office might be going overboard in that direction, minimizing its own responsibility for project content. Evaluators maintained that LWR representatives should be advocating some valid ideas, not merely debating them.

The study recognized that beneficiaries of the LWR programs did include the poor, and that the various communities were helped to become more aware of each other's work. The office was encouraged to make an effort to broaden its own awareness of development lessons and technical information from other parts of the world, and to experiment with creative ways of bringing that information to the various centers. The need was expressed for a closer relationship between regional and New York staff members. Among other recommendations, one urged staff to work with local leaders to define goals more clearly, making it possible to measure progress toward those goals.[21] Still another study, completed in 1990, reaffirmed the effectiveness of the Andean style of accompaniment and partnership.

East Africa Regional Office

The East Africa Regional Office, the second established by LWR, had been in existence for three years when it was first evaluated formally in 1986. Since the underlying purpose of this study was to provide evidence to be used in deciding whether or not the functions of such an office could best be served from Nairobi rather than from New York, the team was composed of persons very familiar with LWR's overall operation. Joseph Sprunger, Robert Cottingham, and Neil Brenden of the New York staff were joined by Harold Hecht, a member of LWR's Board of Directors.

One hesitation in placing a regional office in Nairobi was the fear that its functions might overlap those of international partner agencies with offices already there. This applied principally to Church World Service and the Lutheran World Federation's Department of World Service and Community Development Service. After meeting with representatives of those agencies, the evaluation team determined that an LWR presence in Nairobi actually helped to avoid overlapping and strengthened cooperation through more regular consultation.

The key conclusion was that the office was just beginning to serve its primary purposes: to identify projects directed at the root causes of underdevelopment, to support efforts of local partners to improve their technical and managerial competence, and to foster horizontal linkages between partner agencies and among community groups. Partnership was being fostered through frequent contact; ideas and technical assistance were being shared. Local people believed that a person stationed within the region could better understand their problems, even if that person came from another country.

One perception was clouding the work. Priorities of the regional director, Tom Roach, did not always appear to coincide with New York policies. Local agencies seemed to receive conflicting signals, hearing from New York that LWR was interested only in food production and water resource development, whereas they had been given the impression that there would be support for organizational development and network building. Recommendations were made to honor the representative's judgments and to insure closer coordination in the planning, funding, and monitoring of all projects.

One supplementary function of the office was demonstrated in response to African drought problems. In a relief program for distributing seeds in Kenya, time was of the essence. Because Roach was able overnight to authorize purchase of seeds, they were available in the field in a few days. Seeds purchased just two weeks later arrived too late to germinate.

As a basic finding, the study concluded, "The regional office has projected a presence and provided consultative assistance which simply would not have been done from New York and could not have been done at any lower cost had the persons from New York been available." The team recommended that a regional office of this type should be evaluated every three to five years.[22]

Impressive Statistics

Evaluation could take many different forms. In some cases statistics could demonstrate the effectiveness of a project. This was true in the Maharashtra area of India, where the two married doctors, Rajanikant and Mabelle Arole were at work in the program mentioned in chapter 7. Their Society for Comprehensive Rural Health Projects was devoted to the development of a low-cost, primary health system to be accessible to the poorest of the poor. Since this required empowering people to manage their own affairs, provisions for health care were integrated with programs for socio-economic development. Lutheran World Relief began contributing to the effort in 1977 and the impact is reflected in significant figures. Between 1971 and 1993 the infant mortality rate in the area was reduced from 180 per 1,000 to 19. Deliveries by trained persons increased from 1% to 90%. Immunizations of children rose at the same rate. The birth rate was halved, as the proportion of eligible couples practicing family planning rose from 1% to 60%. Eight thousand artificial limbs and calipers were provided, while nearly 7,000 tuberculosis patients and 4,446 leprosy patients were treated.

In addition to the medical services, 75 women's clubs and 65 young farmers' clubs were organized. Safe drinking water was supplied by 168 new tubewells, 4,500 trees were planted, and 25 plant nurseries were established. LWR's participation contributed significantly to the extension of this effort. The project's value was expanded by the Aroles' influence on public policy throughout India and in other countries.[23]

Continental Comparisons

Not every project could be measured in such statistical terms. A different system for comparing projects within a continent was devised by LWR in the late eighties. In Africa 20 projects from nine countries were included in one study, while in Asia an equal number of projects from six countries were examined. Criteria for ratings were comprehensive, reflecting general purposes of the projects. They were:

1. service to "marginal" community;
2. participants are primary beneficiaries;
3. community participation in decision making;
4. social, economic, and political implications favor primary participants;
5. participation of women evident;
6. use of indigenous resources;
7. technological, cultural, ecological soundness;
8. manageable/sustainable by participants;
9. institution building; and
10. innovative/experimental.

Responses of evaluators were keyed to rate projects as strong, moderate, or not discernible in all categories. In a very few instances the categories were regarded as not applicable.

A project might rate high in all criteria except one, such as innovative/experimental, because it was building on procedures learned from experience elsewhere. On the other hand, if the low rating applied to the category described as participation of women, it was obvious that changes should be considered. A project deficient in categories reflecting community involvement needed thorough re-examination of what was being attempted.[24]

Such evaluations helped staff members to make comparisons among the proposals from various areas and determine priorities. In the early nineties, for example, a decision was made to phase out support for activities in parts of India that had become more advanced, shifting resources to more needy areas.[25]

Participatory Evaluation

While outside experts were often involved in formal evaluations, it was important for project staff members to participate also. In fact, the best evaluation was an ongoing process in which all who were engaged in a project compared intentions with results, learned from experience, identified key weaknesses, and made improvements through changes. Some of the most important achievements, such as enhanced self-worth, could not be reduced to numerical calculations but needed to be taken into account in any meaningful examination.

To facilitate participatory evaluation, Jerry Aaker, who had worked with both Lutheran World Relief and Heifer Project International, led in developing a manual. An early draft was tested in HPI projects in the eighties and a revised version, published in Spanish by Lutheran World Relief in 1989, is widely used in Latin America. The most recent edition, titled, *...Looking Back and Looking Forward...A Participatory Approach to Evaluation*, was published by Heifer Project International in 1994. Aaker summarizes the nature of this type of evaluation:

> The premise of the manual is that ongoing self-evaluation is a participatory learning process. An *ongoing* evaluation system is one in which planning and evaluation proceeds throughout the life of the project, not just at the beginning and end. A *participatory* evaluation system is one that involves

everyone responsible for or interested in the project. Special emphasis is placed on the collaboration of the project organization and the community, with outsider assistance as needed. Evaluation as a *learning process* trains the staff and project participants to systematize their experience, reflect on their results, and plan for future challenges."[26]

Evaluation for the U.S. Government

All of the local and regional efforts in evaluation contributed toward documents required by the U.S. Agency for International Development. Each year LWR was required to submit a detailed report concerning use of the matching grants provided by AID. At the end of 1992, for example, information was submitted concerning the status of 57 projects in nine countries of Latin America, Asia, and Africa. Nearly two million dollars from AID, plus an equal amount of LWR's private matching funds, had been invested in the projects during the preceding four years.

LWR's original proposal to AID had listed three purposes for what was being attempted:

1) support poor partner communities or groups in their effort to meet their own needs as they share in the proposal, design, implementation, evaluation and spread of development endeavors.

2) support the evolution and strengthening of indigenous organizations and development networks capable of and committed to continuing development facilitation beyond the cooperative agreement period.

3) support, complement, and influence development activities of developing countries wherever possible.

A midterm evaluation in 1990 had included visits to 10 project sites, discussions with partner agency staffs and others, and responses to questionnaires from 18 other partners. On the basis of all the accumulated evidence, the evaluators concluded "that LWR is quite capable of meeting all (three) objectives."

The 1992 report reviewed LWR's strategy of helping people find local solutions to their problems. External funding was provided, when necessary, in a way that did not trap the beneficiaries into paying for recurrent costs they could not afford. Since all projects were rooted in communities and not dictated from above, analyses of all 57 projects were submitted. Most of them achieved increased food production, improved health care, progress toward community economic development, and involvement in leadership training. Many other activities had distinctive characteristics due to local conditions.

Examples from Three Continents

From the Mombasa area of Kenya, a project to assist 900 low-income rural women to participate in cooperative groups and activities could report a number of accomplishments. One hundred and one groups had been involved with business and leadership training. All participants received training in project planning, group organization, and business management skills. Fifteen new groups of women established savings clubs, in which activities included raising poultry and goats, making handicrafts, and operating retail shops and tearooms.

In the Cavite region of the Philippines 200 farm families were being helped to realize tangible and significant economic and social development. Financial reports were updated regularly and made available to all cooperative members. During the first of a two-year period, certain measurable targets were achieved: 40% in training people in agroforestry, 73% in livestock raising, 20% in organizational development, and 57% attending pre-membership education classes and training. Virtually all members participated in a goal-setting session on health education. Only 40% of the village council members attended a seminar on village justice.

In Cuzco, Peru, a project was devoted to strengthening rural peasant organizations in defending their interests, elaborating their development alternatives, and participating in regional decision-making processes. Casa Campesina, a meeting point for local authorities and campesinos, had been used by 150,000 people since 1985. A team of 20 community health promoters was supported. Thirty-eight community libraries were undergirding a literacy program. Local leaders were being trained in communal accounting and administration. Two radio programs in Quechua and Spanish were broadcasting topics related to farming and local culture. A legal program provided assistance in land disputes and preparation of community statutes.

A similar project in Ecuador had enabled 81 families, through legal training and defense actions, to obtain rights to 28,000 acres of land.

Summaries of activities by country illustrated the extent of LWR cooperation with local agencies. In India, for example, six partners were involved. Community Action for Social Transformation helped with income-generating schemes, worked with women and youth, carried on programs of primary health care, and planted trees for food and fuel. Christian Council for Rural Development and Research focused on youth employment, women's needs, and community-based health care. Christian Medical Association of India implemented community-based primary health care plans nationwide. Indian Rural Reconstruction Movement worked with local banks to provide loans and implemented health programs. Rural Development Trust involved 151 villagers in social forestry activities, brought 782 into a community credit fund, and established a women's development bank. Comprehensive Rural Health Program trained 37 village health workers and organized 29 women's organizations, beginning a sustainable community-based health and development program among 50,000 people in 60 villages.[27]

Financial Accountability

Detailed financial records were an important part of the document from which the preceding paragraphs were taken. Expenditures for each project were reported. Figures also indicated how funds had been distributed for different purposes. The largest sums were being invested in agricultural development, with health services a strong second. Community development came next, followed by human resources development and institutional development. Allocations from AID, along with LWR matching funds, were listed for each category.

Ample evidence was provided to support the conclusion that costs of the AID-assisted projects were low and the benefits high, not only in terms of economic return on investment, but also in empowerment of people. Most of the projects would need continuing funding for awhile, but there was reason to believe that many of them could become sustainable because of the community structures strengthened to take responsibility.

Through the years Lutheran World Relief has maintained a deserved reputation for exercising good stewardship in its use of resources. The percentage of income allotted for administration has always been low in comparison with other agencies, a fact recognized by such independent evaluators as *Money* magazine.[28] LWR benefited, of course, from the fact that so much of its financial support was raised by church bodies without direct cost to LWR. Expenses were also minimized by the work of countless volunteers in the field. Another factor, emergency relief funding from the U.S. government, sometimes skewed the total expense figures, making administrative overhead appear to be much lower than appropriate or wise under more normal conditions.

Hope Beyond Measurement

Although evaluation teams and statistical reports are valuable, some of the most significant LWR achievements continue to go beyond such measurement and are experienced in the lives of living, hoping people.

A husband in western India, who came home drunk and began to beat his wife for refusing to feed him, was subdued by women in the village who heard her screams. The women locked the man in a room until he sobered up. Later he apologized and promised to remain sober. The women had participated in a two-year program funded by Lutheran World Relief, in which they had learned reading and writing, and gained self-confidence. A similar program in more than 100 Indian villages led to the organization of "mahila mandals," composed of caring women attempting to improve their condition and take an active part in local development programs. Asked about the impact of the "mahila mandal" in her village, one woman replied, "Before this we were like chickens under a basket. Now the basket has been lifted, and we are free." [29]

In Togo, 19 women formed a cooperative to make and market soap in a building they constructed themselves with materials funded by LWR. They work together to get raw materials at bulk rates and technical assistance to improve the quality of the soap. They stamp one side of each bar with their village name, Ave, and the other side with an LWR logo. As they work they sing, "We are women who make soap. We have no fear, women of Ave. Togo, Togo, Togo." [30]

Women are not the only ones needing to have hope restored in many areas where LWR is at work. Men are likely to be depressed by the enormous handicaps confronting their attempts to become self-supporting. LWR's assistance in making water available, improving agriculture, and promoting community development restores the spirit of countless men. In Santiago, Chile, many farmers became able to feed their families because of training they received in organic agriculture from an organization supported by LWR. When Norman

Barth visited the area in 1992 he was told by Osvaldo Gomez, "Today I am a man because I can care for my family." [31]

In Tanzania the birth of a disabled or mentally retarded child was once a family disgrace. Then LWR, with the Evangelical Lutheran Church in Tanzania, arranged for such a family to be given a cow and to be instructed in its care and feeding. The cow provides milk for drinking and manure for a bio-gas generator and the garden. The family's status is elevated to the level of an animal owner and the first calf produced is given to another family with a disabled member. Hope is shared.[32]

Ahead or Behind?

The number of such persons whose hopes have been stirred in partnership with LWR can be multiplied by the hundreds and thousands. But what about the millions? Are we really gaining or losing ground? Are we winning battles while losing the war against hunger and poverty? While LWR is assisting hundreds of villages to make progress toward self-sufficiency, are as many or more becoming less able to take their place in the modern economic order? LWR's 1985 annual report contained the admission, "Moving into its 41st year, LWR faced the reality that poverty, hunger, illiteracy, disease, and early death now affect more people on the planet than ever before." In 1994 a report from three Central American countries served by LWR, Honduras, El Salvador, and Guatemala, was equally pessimistic. Despite large sums of U.S. aid to the area, living standards were lower than in the seventies; the poverty rate, at 70%, was higher; illiteracy, at 50%, was also greater, and the national infrastructures were in worse condition.[33]

With the end of the colonial and cold war periods, during which artificial boundaries forced people from different cultures to live under alien governments, there is bound to be an increase in civil warfare. During such conflicts, when combatants destroy dams and intercept shipments of food, what good is relief? When international fiscal policies lead to enrichment of a few at the expense of many, how can LWR promote empowerment of the poor? Almost daily the public media report dire predictions of economic and environmental disasters. Is Lutheran World Relief prepared to face such a future? Is there really basis for enough hope to combat compassion fatigue? Chapter 11 will deal directly with such questions.

LOCAL PEOPLE were given new hope by digging these wells in Niger (p. 94). More than 3,000 were dug in 10 years.

WHEN WOMEN CHANGE their status for the better, communities improve with them. An agency in southern India brings income and better sanitation.

RUTH AND KEN HELLING organize relief shipments and send out an LWR newsletter in Washington. Such local efforts sustain the agency (p. 109).

MAKING COOKING OIL instead of buying it: Kenyan communities benefit from their own harvest instead of subsidizing others' profits (p. 147).

NORMAN SELL, an LCMS executive, is the board president as LWR celebrates 50 years. Board membership reflects the support of the two largest U.S. Lutheran churches.

WEST AFRICANS, board member Dorothy Raasch and a familiar LWR commodity animate a visit with overseas partners in the 1980s.

"ACCOMPANIMENT" is theme and task for farmer Don Catalino (left) and Kathryn Wolford, now LWR executive director, in Cajamarca, Peru.

NEW CHALLENGES are shaping LWR's future. More than aid is needed to heal Rwanda. Meanwhile these Rwandan refugees in Tanzania now have LWF well water.

LWR in the New World Disorder

In the eighties and nineties dreams of a new world order were replaced by the reality of a new world disorder. Instead of two superpowers challenging one another, clashes—between affluence and poverty, between oppression and freedom—inflamed numerous conflicts throughout the world. Pictures of fleeing refugees and emaciated children from one country after another supplied shocking lead-ins for telecasts. Approaching its fiftieth anniversary, Lutheran World Relief was taking a hard look at its strengths and weaknesses to prepare for what was certain to be a demanding future.

In many situations LWR could follow accepted patterns of work. But new problems, or at least newly intensified ones, grew out of situations where governments, instead of assisting in seeking solutions, might actually be a part of the problem. In country after country, revolutions or civil unrest made relief and development precarious or even unwelcome to existing governments and/or their challengers. Religious fundamentalisms often exacerbated the conflicts, further jeopardizing prospects for LWR service.

Despite such hazards, Lutheran World Relief in the eighties had engaged in significant attempts to minister in the midst of conflicts, and was determined to build on this experience in facing a new world disorder as a new century was approaching.

Blessed Are the Peacemakers

Serving as an agent of healing was not an entirely new function for LWR. Examples of previous involvement included the following:

- Direct assistance to Vietnamese, following the war in their land, was accompanied by attempts to convince the U.S. government to move toward reconciliation.
- LWR partner agencies in Nicaragua, El Salvador, and Guatemala provided a constant prophetic witness for reconciliation in the midst of conflict, seeking to build peace on the foundation of structural changes that would provide for people's basic needs, such as land, education, and health care.

- LWR helped finance a 1989 conference on human rights in Peru, bringing together Peruvian church leaders to discuss violence by the army and the Shining Path guerrillas. LWR later helped to sponsor a similar symposium in Africa.

- The Christian Development Commission in Honduras was provided a grant to foster understanding and to build bridges between Catholics and Protestants.[1]

- In Kenya a project supported by LWR was devoted to ending the cattle theft which was causing violence among the Kuria, Luo, and Masai people in the south Nyanza district. Leaders of hostile groups were encouraged to meet monthly and began engaging in joint activities. Children from the different tribes even sang together in a "Peace Choir" that qualified for national competition.[2]

- In Beit Sahour, Israel, LWR supported a "Palestinian Centre for Rapprochement Between People." Palestinians and Israelis were brought together to engage in dialogue and other activities, attempting to overcome stereotypes, prejudgments, and fears[3]

Chapter 10 reported on the impressive achievement in dealing with the highly publicized Ethiopian famine in the eighties. It was there also that Lutheran World Relief played a pivotal role in a humanitarian effort demonstrating both the possibilities and hazards of involvement in conflict resolution. Periodic famines in Ethiopia, the Sudan, and Somalia were intensified or even created by civil wars. Thousands of refugees streamed back and forth across somewhat artificial borders in the Horn of Africa. The Soviet Union and the U.S. competed for influence in the region.

High-Risk Venture

Lutheran World Relief had an enduring relationship with the Ethiopian Evangelical Church Mekane Yesus, a member of the Lutheran World Federation, and had been providing assistance for many years before the crisis in the eighties. The government in Addis Ababa, known as the Dergue, which had replaced Emperor Haile Selassie in the seventies, was soon facing opposition from different directions. Eritreans could register a historic claim to independence and the United Nations had authorized a federated relationship with Ethiopia, but the provision had been abrogated already in 1962. This action sparked the beginning of 30 years of warfare, undertaken by what became the Eritrean People's Liberation Front. In Tigray similar unrest over the succession of autocratic regimes in Addis Ababa had led to a movement for self-determination which shifted focus over time to advocacy for unity and equality within a federated and decentralized Ethiopia. Other liberation groups, including the Oromo Liberation Front, also emerged.

In an attempt to subdue all such opposition, the Ethiopian government adopted a strategy to multiply the effects of military offensives by damaging or destroying the agricultural and commercial economy of the Eritrean and Tigrayan regions. Land mines were planted, crops and livestock destroyed, wells were poisoned, and markets bombed. Civilians not conscripted were terrorized and sometimes resettled into government-held towns. Every possible attempt was made to restrict the flow of food aid to nongovernment areas. By 1983 Eritrea and Tigray had suffered at least 250,000 casualties, with 500,000 civilians becoming refugees in Sudan. Thousands more were internally displaced.

Both the Eritrean and Tigrayan liberation groups established their own agencies to relieve the suffering of their people. These were not directly controlled by the military but dependent on its active cooperation. All such attempts labored under severe handicaps. Offensives surged back and forth; territory under the control of the insurgents was sometimes limited and scattered. Internal resources were scarce, and initial pleas to agencies already providing aid to areas under government control produced little response.

Representatives of the United Nations were unwilling to challenge the concept of the absolute sovereignty of a member. The World Council of Churches and the Lutheran World Federation were reluctant to assist the liberation groups for fear of government reprisal on a member church (although the Lutheran Church in Eritrea was also a member of the LWF). Even the Red Cross would not assist in areas uncontrolled by the government. But the Sudan Council of Churches and seven European agencies, led by Norwegian Church Aid, began delivering cross-border humanitarian assistance into the war-ravaged areas in the late seventies. When an actual ecumenical consortium was established in 1981, Lutheran World Relief was the only American organization to join what was called the Emergency Relief Desk, operating out of Khartoum, Sudan. Canadian Lutheran World Relief and the Mennonite Central Committee did not begin participating until the end of the decade. Lutheran World Relief's access to U.S. aid, added to its contributions from private sources, provided resources which, by 1985, exceeded the contributions from all other countries for the bold operation.[4]

Food shipments were routed through Port Sudan on the Red Sea and, later, through the Ethiopian port of Massawa. Sudan allowed most of this aid to go through its territory across borders into Eritrea and Tigray. In one year alone, 1990, LWR provided enough food to meet the emergency dietary needs of more than 1.5 million people in the two areas. Trucks, provided by both U.S. and private funds, transported the aid under cover of night over roads dug and maintained by hand, subject to daily bombings and strafing by government air forces.[5] Meanwhile, liberation forces also attacked garrison towns, disrupting relief operations in government areas. There was even controversy between relief agencies serving government areas and the Emergency Relief Desk's cross-border operation as to which effort was serving the most people. According to one estimate, the Ethiopian government at one time had access to only 22% of civilians at risk.

Dilemma and Resolution

As fighting continued, LWR staff struggled with the question, "Are we a positive or negative factor in the Ethiopian equation?" LWR had a valid claim to political neutrality, since assistance was being given to suffering people on both sides of the battle fronts. Aid was still channeled through the LWF to Ethiopians under government control. Although the Eritrean and Tigrayan movements were split for several years on both military strategy and ideological differences, LWR continued serving both of those groups through the Emergency Relief Desk. But any aid to the insurgents could be seen as a means for prolonging the war. Providing for civilian needs relieved pressure on liberation forces to feed civilians, allowing them to devote more resources to the military and increasing their determination to prevail. Recognizing this reality, LWR advocated a "tough love" policy within the consortium, arguing that continued aid should be linked with encouragement to participate in peace initiatives. The U.S. government was also urged to take this position in conversations with all combatants, including the Ethiopian government.[6]

The fortunes of war shifted back and forth, but toward the end of the eighties the liberation fronts began to make significant advances, while internal opposition to the Dergue also increased. The Eritreans captured Massawa in February, 1990, and Asmara on May 25, 1991. The Ethiopian People's Revolutionary Democratic Front marched into Addis Ababa three days later, and an uneasy peace replaced thirty years of war. Two years later Eritrea became a sovereign nation and the Tigrayans and Oromos were participants in a new Ethiopian government. The extent of Lutheran World Relief's influence in ending that war is a subject for historical analysis, but there is no doubt that a contribution was made. In 1986 LWR became the first church-related relief and development agency to receive the Presidential End Hunger Award. The citation, signed by Ronald Reagan, recognized the broad scope of LWR's work in dealing with emergencies, undertaking sustainable development, and educating the public on hunger issues, but made special reference to LWR's role in "aiding victims of famine on both sides of the Ethiopian civil war." [7]

In 1991 the Relief Society of Tigray awarded a certificate to LWR "as an acknowledgement of the humanitarian concern and commitment in alleviating the problems caused by natural and man-made disasters for which the people of Tigray are deeply grateful." [8]

Reflecting on this experience, Norman Barth said, "The efforts of relief agencies are noble and necessary, but they are not enough. Such agencies must also become involved in the more difficult task of securing peace." [9] LWR added to its policy guidelines an authorization to support projects which "provide a reconciling and healing ministry in situations where the aspirations of the poor and oppressed in less developed countries are frustrated by social conflict and war." [10]

Humanitarianism in Wartime

Lutheran World Relief's determination to serve victims on both sides of a conflict was shared by other relief and development agencies. In 1989, during the Sudanese civil war, the international community launched Operation Lifeline Sudan to provide aid to people under siege. As in Ethiopia, combatants were disrupting relief efforts until the United Nations negotiated with the government of the Sudan and the Sudan People's Liberation Movement and Army to allow humanitarian assistance to use designated corridors to reach civilians on either side of the conflict. This agreement was not always respected and countless complications interfered with the operation. Lifeline had no mandate to end war but did play a role in creating "an environment for peace." The Lifeline story is significant and has been reported in detail by Larry Minear. [11]

Drawing on such experiences in a number of countries, Minear became codirector of the Humanitarianism and War Project, relating practice to theory. From that research effort has come a handbook, a "work in progress," analyzing humanitarian issues and making recommendations to improve humanitarian programs. Proposed guideposts include these:

- Humanitarian action responds to human suffering because people are in need.... It should not take sides in conflict.
- To fulfill their mission, humanitarian organizations should be free of interference from home or host political authorities.
- For effective humanitarian action, encouraging respect for human rights and addressing underlying causes of conflicts are essential elements.
- Where humanitarianism and sovereignty clash, sovereignty should defer to the relief of life-threatening suffering.[12]

Whatever the merits and hazards of engaging in conflict resolution, one result for a participating agency is to be in a favorable position, after the war, to be welcomed by survivors to join in the massive effort needed for rehabilitation. During the rebuilding attempted in Nicaragua after the civil war there, reconciling efforts were regarded by LWR staff members as "an investment in an early return to the longer-term tasks of reconstruction and development." An issue paper included the additional comment, "As long as the animosities which played themselves out in warfare remain, the achievement of the God-given potential to which LWR is committed will not be realized."[13]

When the Conflict No Longer Makes the Headlines

After U.S. soldiers left Somalia in 1993, there was little media coverage of what was happening there. But LWR stayed and invested heavily in the Baidoa area of the country. Much of the expenditure was devoted to the rehabilitation of water pumps and wells. LWR had been in Somalia since 1980 and, as in so many countries, had worked with the people to develop essential supplies of water. During the fighting, marauders had poured gasoline on many wells and melted down the pumps. The residents of one village, hearing what had happened elsewhere, dismantled their pump and hid the parts in the bushes before fleeing; only a few elders remained. When the bandits arrived, they confronted the elders, demanding to be told where the parts had been hidden. Four chiefs refused and were executed before one revealed the location of the parts, which were stolen and sold. In at least one other village the same practice of hiding the parts was successful and, when the fighting was over, the pump and well were easily returned to service.[14]

During the conflict many Somali had been herded into emergency feeding centers, but rehabilitating the water supplies made it possible for the people to go back to their villages, rebuild their houses, and replant their fields. LWR engaged in the same type of water rehabilitation program necessitated by the war in the Sudan.

Achievements in countries like Somalia and the Sudan are anything but a cause for complacency; there is not even assurance of effective governments after the end of the military conflicts. The result of relief and development efforts often constitutes a reprieve, not a solution. After LWR had been in Somalia for only a short time, in 1982, a section in the agency's Annual Report headed, LONG-TERM SOLUTIONS, included the observation that the situation in that country was "a good example of how LWR is helping solve not just immediate but intermediate and long-term problems." Within a decade Somalia was a disaster area. Long-term problems are often addressed without being solved. Starvation recurs periodically in a number of countries.

From Africa to Asia to Latin America, the global spotlight moves across areas of poverty and unrest. Along with partners around the world, LWR struggles to discover what more can be done, realistically, to deal with long-term problems.

The Doom Boom

At the end of the twentieth century, flammable elements of overpopulation, resource depletion, and floods of refugees are being ignited by a succession of military conflicts. During the Cold War there was always the threat of global catastrophe but, meanwhile, the opposing superpowers maintained a semblance of order within their own spheres of influence. Now, in one country after another, there are devastating bloodbaths with little mediating pressure from outside sources. Because many of them intensify tribal antagonisms, the tendency among the wealthier countries is to regard them as evidence of a primitive bloodlust and simply to wait for the anarchy to burn itself out.

This superficial analysis disregards the real causes of both the poverty and the violence. One Nigerian writer expressed the consensus of many experts:

There is only one root source of the violence: more and more people are competing for fewer and fewer resources. The struggle for ever scarcer resources—and as a direct consequence for political power—is what fuels conflicts in Rwanda, Burundi and elsewhere in Africa. The real problems are economic and social ones, not tribalism.[15]

Tipped Scales

Working with the poorest of the poor, LWR became painfully aware of the economic handicaps facing developing nations. In international trade, scales were weighted against them. Tanzanian cotton was bought in Europe and North America at such prices that the growers could not afford to buy the manufactured blue jeans. Similarly, growers of the raw material for rope could not afford to buy the rope produced abroad. When Tanzanians decided to manufacture the rope locally and market it themselves, they discovered that the rate per pound on the shipping was five times as much for the finished rope as it was for the raw material.[16]

In an attempt to make headway in the international economic competition the developing nations borrowed heavily, but this often extended the inequities. Some of the loans were devoted to such capital-intensive enterprises that only the affluent were aided.

Provisions for repayment were unrealistic. Norman Barth reported to the directors in 1993: "The developing world owes the North about $1.3 trillion. Each year the interest and capital repayment (if any is possible) amounts to $150 billion, about three times what the developing nations receive in aid. Yet the American public still perceives the flow of resources as going from North to South, rather than the opposite.... Debt is the new slavery that is shackling the nations in the South." [17] Barth had written President Reagan in July, 1988, proposing that much of the debt owed to the United States by poor African nations be converted from loans to grants. He maintained, "The cost of such conversion to the U.S. taxpayer will be slight compared to the potential cost to the United States and the global economy resulting from the stagnant economic conditions in Africa and the possible economic collapse of many states on that continent."[18] By 1994 debts in Latin America also were so great that those countries were described as becoming "Africanized."

Although Lutheran World Relief's fundamental reason for concern over such economic injustice was always in the biblical identification of a neighbor as any person in need, Norman Barth also saw an interplay between domestic and foreign needs. He pointed to certain American problems that could only be addressed by better cooperation with developing nations. The drug flow to this country has been due partly to the inability of poor farmers in the drug-producing areas to grow and market more profitable legal crops. The threat of depressed wages and escalating costs of social services from the flow of illegal immigrants could be reduced by helping countries to move toward sustained economic development to provide employment for their citizens.

Barth posed the question, "What better serves our national domestic interests—-narrow, introverted, parochial programs only, or a genuine concern to contribute to a robust sustainable economy in the South?" He was convinced that LWR needed to be more active in advocacy and development education for social change.[19]

New Impetus for Tradition

Advocacy was not a new function for LWR in the eighties. In its first year Lutheran World Relief had been active in bringing about a change in U.S. policy toward Germany. Shortly before his death in 1979 Paul Empie told an interviewer, "I have said over and over again and will go to my grave saying it that love and justice are two sides of the same coin. If I say I love my brother and will not lift my finger to secure justice for him, I'm a liar and a hypocrite." [20] The Office on Development Policy has always engaged actively in deliberations concerning national and global efforts toward justice. Cheryl Morden from that office provided leadership and participated with representatives of 44 other agencies in a coalition that developed a document proposing new directions for U.S. economic policy toward Central America.[21]

Through the years LWR offered informed advice and took positions on many issues. Attention was directed regularly to unjust conditions in Latin America. In 1981 directors noted the "rising tide of torture and violence, especially in El Salvador and Guatemala," and expressed concern over "the readiness of our government to provide arms which often serve to support groups which have killed church and community leaders as well as U.S. citizens, while rejecting offers for negotiated settlement." [22] In 1983, when a Lutheran pastor, Medardo Gomez, and a physician serving in a refugee camp, Angel Ibarra, were arrested for "associating with subversives" in San Salvador, Robert

Busche mobilized representatives from many agencies to join in pressing the government to release them. Both were physically abused, but Gomez was freed within 48 hours and Ibarra was released months later after continuing interrogation and torture.[23] In 1985 LWR joined other voluntary agencies in reminding the U.S. government that aid to the contras in Nicaragua violated international law barring the sending of humanitarian aid to fighting forces.[24]

Concern for justice was applied to Lutheran World Relief's own projects. In 1983, for example, directors determined to support no projects that would be supported by either the South African government or its nominally independent tribal homelands. Their resolution also stated that approved projects "should not enhance apartheid either philosophically or in practice." [25]

Similar attention was given by LWR to many other specific issues, but always there was the need to encourage the U.S. government to allocate aid on the basis of need rather than on fluctuating political factors. In the nineties Israel and Egypt continued to receive their annual allocation of $5.1 billion while more needy nations went begging. The division of the 5.1 billion also reflected political calculation, since Egypt, with 10 times the population of Israel, received only two-thirds of the amount of aid going to Israel. In 1994 the impending catastrophe in Rwanda escalated while the more affluent nations paid little attention because the country was politically insignificant. It was the churches of the world that finally focused attention on what had become a scandal of genocide.

Concern for Justice Begins at Home

During a conference conducted under LWR auspices on the subject, "The Challenge of the Poor to Christians in Affluence," one participant was baffled. She said, "Nobody in this country writes a policy that says, 'I'm going to step on poor people.' How can I help?" Among the speakers who had prompted the woman's question, the development secretary of a Tanzanian Lutheran church had said, "You continue to help us in charity, but until there are structural and political changes, we will continue to struggle for years and years." The woman's question expressed the frustration of many faithful supporters of Lutheran World Relief.[26] Accepting the judgment of devoted LWR staff members that concerned citizens should be involved in influencing national policies, it is natural for constituents to wonder where a person should begin. Staff members, certainly including those in the Office on Development Policy, harbor a related frustration. They wonder how their work can be strengthened by enlisting the participation of the millions of church members.

Jerry Aaker is one of a number of development professionals who maintain that global, sustainable development will be achieved only by "transformation," which involves changes in the individual, as well as changes in the institutions and structures of society in both the developed and developing nations. The goal of transformation is nothing less than the creation of new and just social relationships. To Aaker transformation is the essence of the biblical, "At the moment your surplus meets their need, but one day your need may be met from their surplus. The aim is equality; as Scripture has it, 'the one who got much had no more than enough, and the one who got little did not go short.'" [27]

To some people the concept of transformation sounds so formidable as to discourage financial contributions. Instead, however, persons motivated to contribute may be just the ones to grasp a larger vision of stewardship. At any rate, the policy of Lutheran World Relief has always been to combine financial appeals with an effort to inform and motivate constituents concerning a global strategy. Dealing with global poverty requires alerting members of our churches to the ways in which we are depleting such vital resources as forests, fossil fuels, farmlands, and even our atmospheric shield.

Fortunately, LWR has enjoyed cooperation with many others in this effort. The world relief/world hunger programs of the LCMS and the ELCA not only raise funds for basic support of LWR but carry on an extensive educational ministry, addressing justice issues and urging lifestyle simplification.

Educating individuals to engage in political advocacy raises few objections. For official agencies of a church to take political stands is another matter; most opposition can be overcome by establishing a policy requiring formal action by a governing body before advocacy is approved. Since, however, LWR is a separate corporation with access to relevant data concerning global needs and government policies, church officials generally welcome LWR intervention. Al Senske, director of LCMS World Relief, said, "I rejoice in the fact that statements on public policy can be made through both Lutheran World Relief and Lutheran Immigration and Refugee Service." [28]

The line between advocacy and lobbying is often fuzzy, but LWR does not endanger its status with the Internal Revenue Service as an organization to which contributions are tax-deductible. The cost of all of LWR's attempts to influence public policy is a tiny fraction of the agency's expenses, well below the percentage allowing organizations with budgets as large as LWR's to assure constituents of the agency's IRS status.

LWR's most influential partner in the hunger/politics arena is certainly Bread for the World (BFW), founded in 1973 by a Lutheran pastor, Arthur Simon, and led since 1991 by another Lutheran, David Beckmann. From its beginning BFW has acknowledged its biblical roots and is supported by a wide range of Christians. Bread for the World devotes most of its work to influencing public policy, making contributions for that purpose nondeductible according to Internal Revenue provisions.

The "Voiceless" Speak for Themselves

In dealing with poverty and oppression, humanitarian agencies first saw themselves as the "voice of the voiceless." Today, with the emergence of new sectors of civil society, including women and environmental groups, LWR partners are no longer voiceless; they can articulate not only needs but also constructive alternatives and policy. The role of LWR now is to amplify the voices and to open access to global policy makers.

In an attempt to impress global financial agencies, governments in some developing countries have adopted financial policies that increase hardship for the poor. Farmers are recruited to raise cash crops which provide exports but leave the growers impoverished and even without food for themselves. Industrial development is subsidized, enriching the elite but taking money from social programs originally intended to help the poor survive. The landless and unemployed pour into the cities, enlarging the slums.

Wherever LWR is involved, attempts are made to empower people to participate in the governance of their society. Carol Capps, from the Office on Development Policy, participated in the planning of a conference in Tanzania in 1990 bringing 400 participants from 38 countries to devote five days to formulating an "African Charter for Popular Participation in Development and Transformation." The document was transmitted to heads of governments and the U.N. General Assembly. Capps spearheaded follow-up work in helping Africans shed the "dependency syndrome" and become self-reliant through participation in the decision-making process.[29] LWR's East African Regional Office stays in touch with partner agencies concerning their experience with political and economic reforms. The Malagasy Lutheran Church and the Christian Council of Mozambique report dramatic political changes in those countries. People in Mali, Niger, and Burkina Faso have experienced the power of working together to influence public officials.[30] In a number of localities LWR provides assistance to victims whose legal rights have been violated.

Preserving the Resource Base

Encouraging local empowerment includes working with partners to confront the danger of exhausting available resources. A report issued to the General Assembly of the United Nations in 1987, "Our Common Future," proposed long-term environmental strategies for achieving "sustainable development, reversing the trend to deplete the forests, fuels, tillable soil, wildlife, and oxygen supplies." LWR subscribed to the document, regarding its implications as "clearly the business of the church." [31]

This was not really anything new for LWR, but it gave stimulation to an ongoing effort. In places like Mali, Burkina Faso, and Niger, LWR assisted partners in resisting the creeping inroad of the desert by gardening, composting, reforesting, planting live fences, and erecting firebreaks. Similar efforts have been directed to restoring denuded forests and improving marginal farmland in remote hills of India.[32]

In El Salvador and Nicaragua farmers learned to replace the use of chemical fertilizers and pesticides with ecologically sound agricultural techniques. Natural pesticides made from neem trees proved to be more effective than chemical products. The planting of nitrogen-fixing beans and the application of organic compost resulted in gardens overflowing with vegetables on land which had become unproductive soil. Bordering the gardens, marigolds and herbal plants provided a scent which repelled harmful worms and insects, eliminating the need for chemical pesticides.[33]

In Mindanao, Philippines, a project joined LWR with local tribes in halting the erosion brought about by traditional slash-and-burn cultivation practices. Overcultivation had also depleted the soil's fertility. Erosion control measures were adopted and diversified farming begun; logging was banned. As elsewhere, these efforts were accompanied by educational experiences and moves toward community development. In this instance there was even a major step in the direction of empowerment. Since the tribes were living on land designated as a public forest, families were allocated five acres each, and applications submitted for 25-year renewable land leases to give the farmers new security. More than 150 such certificates have been obtained, with approval for more pending.[34]

Relief, development, leadership cultivation, community empowerment, concern for peace and justice, conflict resolution, advocacy; by whatever terms, LWR's agenda had expanded during fifty years and new leaders would be confronted with a wide range of prospects and problems.

New Leadership for a New Century

To guide LWR's transition from one century to another, a new executive and a new president were elected. Norman Barth, who had fine-tuned the administration of the agency and extended its vision, retired in 1993. His knowledge of governmental affairs had helped to prepare LWR staff to deal with the kind of international issues that were becoming increasingly relevant to LWR activities. His successor, Kathryn Wolford, had first-hand experience in accompaniment and advocacy. She had worked with Church World Service for nine years in the Caribbean and Washington, D.C., before becoming LWR program director for Latin America in 1991.

Robert Marshall, who had been an LWR board member since 1968 and president since 1979, retired from both positions in January, 1994. He had worked so closely with Norman Barth that, on occasion, they had issued joint statements. In LWR's 1991 report they had looked into LWR's future and said:

> The next decade will witness the birth of 850 million people in the developing world. Most will be born poor and grow up in poverty. However, they will retain the hope that eventually their condition will change for the better. Hope is a major force in the lives of people in the developing world. Hope challenges the future to outdo the past. The mission of Lutheran World Relief...is to help people turn hope into reality.... LWR strives not only to bring a more productive existence to people in the developing world but also to lift them to the point where they are more in line with God's plan for all.

Marshall was thoroughly familiar with LWR's wide range of endeavors and could bring to deliberations a global perspective informed by his active participation in the work of the Lutheran World Federation. He had special concern for the Palestinians in Israel's West Bank and Gaza, whose needs were so often overlooked by the rest of the world. Marshall's ability to unravel the strands of complex issues made him an effective presiding officer and an influential advocate on behalf of LWR with both church and state. His long and close association with staff members motivated him to write, in his final comments for the 1993 Annual Report, "We who monitor the programs and the management of funds, which our church members provide to LWR, are fully assured that we have an enviable staff of capable professionals. All of them are dedicated to pouring themselves out, often away from home for weeks, conferring for long hours, prayerfully assessing opportunities and then recommending actions and working with fellow humans the world over to develop new hope."

Marshall's confidence in the LWR staff was encouraging to his successor, Norman D. Sell, who was vice-president for finance and treasurer of The Lutheran Church—Missouri Synod. Sell, the first representative from LCMS to be president, and Wolford, the first woman to be executive director, symbolized the breadth of LWR's constituency.

Sell had been an LWR Director since 1988 and had served as a board member of the Lutheran Council in the U.S.A. from 1978 to 1983. His experience included years in private industry, state government, and administration of higher education. Looking toward his new role, Sell indicated that he planned to operate primarily as chairman of the board, rather than as president. Expecting the board to concentrate on policy-making, he would preside over deliberations on those matters, but he would expect the positions and functions of LWR to be articulated by the chief staff person, the executive director.[35]

In a statement to the directors prior to her election Wolford had made clear that she was comfortable with the directions taken in recent years by Lutheran World Relief. She wrote, "We are called to not only alleviate the suffering of victims of oppression and structural injustice, but also to transform those relationships and structures which impoverish, marginalize and dehumanize people. That begins with a process of self-examination about our individual stewardship and that of the corporate structures to which we belong, in relation to the needs of the global community." [36]

Vision for Vitality

Soon after her election, Wolford consulted with staff colleagues about the agency's future, and there was general agreement that LWR is poised for flexible action in accompanying partners to realize hopes for their communities' personal, economic, and political development. LWR is obviously capable of assisting with sustainable, ecologically sound food production, health care, literacy education, and strengthening the institutional capacities of grassroots agencies. Women and children warrant special attention, not only because they remain the most vulnerable in much of the world, but because help for women means help for the whole family. Efforts that empower people and communities to reach their full human potential are fundamental. Contributing to peace and reconciliation will be as demanding as it is essential.

Decisions concerning specific directions to be taken are to be made in partnership with overseas organizations and those they serve. In this process, sharing and learning will continue to occur among LWR offices, overseas partners, U.S. constituency, and others involved in the broad sphere of international cooperation.[37]

Vision must take into account financial realities. Support for LWR, while reliable, has not been expanding along with perceived needs. Many congregations are entrusting a declining portion of their income to denominational offices, but contributing to outreach efforts in which they sense more direct involvement.

Comparison of LWR's annual expenditures is not very helpful because those figures are sometimes distorted by huge government emergency grants. In 1993, a relatively "normal" year, LWR's total income slightly exceeded 24 million dollars. Six million, or 26%, came directly from church sources, four million, or 17%, from individual and corporate gifts, many of which have Lutheran origin, and more than 10 million, 43%, represented the value of gifts-in kind, such as medicine, quilts, and clothing. More than three million, 14%, came from government grants, chiefly for relief of the African drought. LWR is reassessing the possibility of seeking AID funding for a few specific projects. LWR's relationship with the churches, however, continues to be a very influential factor in the agency's future.

LWR and Christian Faith

Kathryn Wolford has stated from the beginning that she shares with directors and staff colleagues the determination for LWR to continue to be an authentic expression of Christian faith. She opened her initial statement to the directors with Luke's quotation from Jesus' sermon in Nazareth focused on concern for the poor, the captives, the blind, and the oppressed, and said, "Acts of mercy, compassion and justice are intimately related to our Christian faith. Imitating, however imperfectly, the healing, reconciling and transforming ministry of Jesus is an act of discipleship. It is our individual responsibility as Christians and our corporate responsibility as the Church to serve people in need throughout the world." [38]

For half a century all LWR leaders have voiced similar convictions. LWR's distinctive expression of the faith has been to serve on the basis of need alone, not necessarily connected with verbal proclamation of the gospel. Director Leslie Weber once said, "By and large the person in the pew in LCMS wants to help people who are hurting.... They are filled with the kind of compassion that Jesus had, and that we want all Christians to have." [39]

Wherever government funds are involved in a relief project, there can be no explicit appeal to faith, but LWR workers regard such a combination as unwise communication strategy anyway. It is important to make clear that LWR is not attempting to use food and clothing to seduce people into becoming "rice Christians."

The persons serving give witness to their faith in nonverbal ways: through their compassion, the quality of their work, their embodiment of values, and recognition of spiritual needs. This has been enough to encourage LWR representatives laboring in difficult situations. Edwin Moll, even when frustrated by conditions in Palestine, could write: "We do have the intense satisfaction that our Christian witness, manifested through our love-deeds and gifts, is making a sure and constantly deeper impression upon formerly hostile hearts. We have saved many, many lives; we have relieved so infinitely much suffering and misery—and we are doing it, always in His beloved name and for His sake." [40]

Although LWR workers do not ordinarily initiate verbal witness, they are ready to answer questions about their motivation, and they are often given this opportunity. There have been occasions in both Africa and Asia when persons asking to be baptized have been urged to delay this action until they have had time to gain an understanding of the full nature of the Christian faith. [41] Lutherans also know that the accomplishment of God's will is not dependent entirely on human actions. The Spirit often moves in ways beyond our comprehension.

In many countries where LWR is at work it is possible to count on local channels, Lutheran or ecumenical, to supplement the ministry of service with the ministry of the Word. In Latin America, where 99% of the people are Roman Catholics, one Lutheran missionary told Robert Busche, "The primary job that Christians here have is to help people to renew and live out their baptismal covenant." [42] In Nicaragua and Honduras there is more cooperation between the historical Protestant churches and the so-called Evangelicals than in the U.S. [43]

Not all nations, however, permit Christian churches to function in freedom within their territory. Granted that there is a valid ministry of "hands" as well as of "mouth," and that LWR's primary function is the former, is this ever enough by itself? This question naturally recurs among persons who believe that there is something distinctive about the "abundant life" that goes beyond "bread alone" and is so valuable that appreciating it requires sharing it. Looking only at ourselves, we may be satisfied in a ministry confined to service, but considering the needs of the other person, can we settle for the ministry of hands alone any more than we can settle for relief alone? Periodically, thoughtful constituents, staff members, and directors have questioned decisions concerning location of LWR projects. Limited resources require setting priorities among the almost unlimited places where work is needed. Should projects be undertaken in lands where there are no churches and where evangelism is forbidden?

Executives devoted to the totality of mission give at least one reason for venturing into lands where such conditions prevail. The fact that LWR is allowed to undertake a social ministry in a country where the church is otherwise excluded makes it possible to correct images of Christianity as a partner in imperialism and exploitation. Once in Jerusalem Edwin Moll introduced S. C. Michelfelder to a Muslim official, who volunteered, "We do not understand the kind of Christianity that fights for the Holy Places in our land. But we do understand your kind of Christianity, and you will be interested to know that my son is attending one of your schools. I want him to know about that kind of Christianity also." [44]

A similar observation was made in Bangladesh, where LWR participated in a massive LWF program of relief and development when the country, previously known as East Pakistan, became independent in the seventies. At a dinner celebrating the transfer of church-related relief activities back to local leadership, the Minister of Social Affairs in the new government, a Muslim, said:

I find it difficult to understand you people and your work. In the midst of our trauma and suffering we needed help.... Our whole country and its government had to be rebuilt. Then who came to show their good will and provide assistance to our people? Was it the people of the various religions in neighboring countries——the Hindus, the Buddhists, or the people from China? Or Japan? Or was it our fellow Muslims from South Asia or the Near East? No, it was you Christians——you whose representatives in Bangladesh don't even number one percent of our population. What made you do this? What motivated you to come and help us? Even though your action is hard to understand, we do appreciate it and want to express our deepest gratitude to you.[45]

Beyond 1995

Fifty years ago Lutherans found in their faith the courage and determination to help millions of people survive the ravages of war. Today millions more are threatened by hunger and poverty, intensified by military, political, and economic conflicts.

In such a predicament it is natural to think that we cannot make a difference. Persons acting only out of good will may be discouraged by the enormity of global need; compassion fatigue sets in when results do not meet expectations.

But Lutherans have the best reasons for not being dismayed. We are not preoccupied with success, nor are we even striving to win God's favor, because we know that we are loved unconditionally. Motivated by the desire to respond to that love, we welcome the opportunity to join our Lord in tasks to be completed in God's good time. We can take risks not conditioned by fear of failure; we need only be faithful. That conviction inspired LWR's founders. The story of Lutheran World Relief shows how individuals, working together in communities and partnerships spanning the globe, can make a real difference.

The faith we share today with LWR's founders reminds us that "we have not been given the spirit of fear, but of power, and of love, and of discipline." Lutheran World Relief enlists the power of a loving people in the discipline of discipleship. That truth is the driving force behind LWR's move into the next century.

Notes

Introduction: Hope Confronts Despair

1. *World Economic Survey*, United Nations, 1993.
2. S. C. Michelfelder, NLC *News Bureau*, November 26, 1945.

Chapter 1: A Family Crisis

1. Osborne Hauge, *Lutherans Working Together*, NLC, 1949, p.63.
2. Rollin Shaffer, "LWA—a Quarter Century of Christian Compassion," *National Lutheran*, December, 1965, and January, 1966.
3. "We Saw Europe," NLC *News Bureau*, May, 1945.
4. Michael Markel, Oral History, p.4, ELCA Archives.
5. C. E. Krumbholz, letter to American Council of Voluntary Agencies, December 11, 1945, ELCA Archives.
6. Minutes, NLC Division of Welfare, January 21, 1946.
7. Hallie Baker Confer, interview by author, September 23, 1993.
8. NLC *News Bureau*, November 12, 1945.
9. Oswald C. J. Hoffman in "Franklin Clark Fry, A Palette for a Portrait," edited by Robert H. Fischer, *The Lutheran Quarterly*, Volume XXIV, 1972, p. 208.
10. Minutes, LWR, April 2, 1946.
11. Paul Empie, letter to Lutherans, October 29, 1945, ELCA Archives.
12. NLC *News Bureau*, December 4, 1945.
13. Minutes, LWR, March 29, 1946.
14. NLC *News Bureau*, April 13, 1945.

Chapter 2: The German Question

1. NLC *News Bureau*, December 4, 1945.
2. Krumbholz letter to Long, November 19, 1945, ELCA Archives.
3. NLC *News Bureau*, December 29, 1945.
4. Harpers, N.Y. and London, 1946.
5. Empie in NLC *News Bureau*, December 5, 1945.
6. "Franklin Clark Fry, a Palette for a Portrait," *The Lutheran Quarterly*, Volume XXIV, 1972, pp.171-172.
7. Otto Piper, open letter, February 12, 1946, ELCA Archives,
8. Fry, letter and statement, October 17, 1947, ELCA Archives.
9. Merle Miller, *Plain Speaking*, Putnam's Sons, N.Y., 1973, pp. 240-247.
10. Concordia Publishing House, 1992.
11. Minutes, LWR, 1946-50.
12. Letter, July 17, 1947, ELCA Archives.
13. Letter, March 7, 1948, ELCA Archives.
14. Letter, Yaeger to Confer, June 12, 1950, ELCA Archives.
15. Letter, Lilje to Long, March 24, 1947, ELCA Archives.
16. Scherzer, Oral History, p. 4, ELCA Archives.
17. Richard Solberg, *As Between Brothers*, Augsburg Publishing House, 1957, p. 31.
18. Mau, interview by author, November 18, 1993.
19. Letter, Hennings to Brown, December 13, 1946, ELCA Archives.
20. Mau, interview by author, November 18, 1993.
21. NLC *News Bureau*, January 10, 1947.
22. Nielsen, Oral History, p. 7, ELCA Archives.

23. Internal LWR memos, March, 1948, ELCA Archives.
24. NLC *News Bureau*, April 7, 1949.
25. Solberg, *As Between Brothers*, Augsburg, 1957, pp. 65-67.
26. *National Lutheran*, Spring, 1946, p. 1.
27. Eileen Egan and Elizabeth Clark Reiss, *Transfigured Night, The CRALOG Experience*, Livingston, Phil.-N.Y., 1964, pp. 84-88.
28. Nerger, interview by author, September 1, 1993.
29. Letter, Confer to Moll, August 16, 1949, ELCA Archives.
30. NLC *News Bureau*, November 30, 1945.

Chapter 3: Extended Need, Expanded Partnership

1. Hallie Baker Confer, interview by author, September 23, 1993, and letter, Confer to Yaeger, January 9, 1950, ELCA Archives.
2. Annual Report, NLC, 1951, p. 27.
3. Empie, *Inside LWA*, Lutheran World Action, 1970, p. 5.
4. "LCMS Response to World Hunger," internal paper, 1993.
5. Nielsen, Oral History, p. 23, ELCA Archives.
6. Annual Report, LWR, 1955, p. 346.
7. NLC *News Bureau*, November 30, 1959.
8. Ibid., December 17, 1951.
9. Dagny Schiotz, interview by author, December 14, 1993.
10. Annual Report, LWR, 1958, p. 171.
11. Nielsen, Oral History, p. 23, ELCA Archives.

Chapter 4: Lutheran WORLD Relief

1. NLC *News Bureau*, May 22, 1957, and July, 1960.
2. Nerger interview by author, September 1, 1993.
3. NLC *News Bureau*, September 10, 1953.
4. Confer correspondence, 1955, ELCA Archives, and Claypool interview by author, January 7, 1994.
5. NLC *News Bureau*, May 20, 1954.
6. Ibid., October 6, 1959.
7. Ibid., February 19, 1953; May 27, 1953; October 24, 1957; June 26, 1958.
8. Ibid., February 19, 1958.
9. Ibid., February 6, 1958.
10. Ibid., September 5, 1958.
11. Ibid., August 2, 1955.
12. Ibid., January 14, 1952.
13. Ibid., July 10, 1959.

Chapter 5: Checkpoint

1. Internal document, Office of Finance and Administration, LWR.
2. NLC *News Bureau*, April 22, 1959.
3. Nielsen, Oral History, p. 49, ELCA Archives.
4. Annual Report, LWR, 1965, and NLC *News Bureau*, March 10, 1961.
5. NLC *News Bureau*, September 1, 1960.
6. Policy statement attached to Annual Report, LWR, 1961.
7. *National Lutheran*, January, 1963, p. 6.
8. Ibid., February, 1963, p. 7.

9. Empie, Oral History, p.115, ELCA Archives.
10. Oral Histories, Confer, pp. 94-97, and Nielsen, pp. 28-29, ELCA Archives plus interviews with others by author.
11. "A Critical Review," in minutes, LWR, March 29, 1963.
12. Empie, Annual Report, LWR, 1970.
13. Empie, Oral History, pp. 49-50, ELCA Archives.
14. Minutes, LWR, November 24, 1969, Exhibit H.
15. Ibid., June 30, 1965.
16. NLC *News Bureau*, February 24 and August 13, 1964.

Chapter 6: Beyond Relief

1. NLC *News Bureau*, December 5, 1961.
2. Ibid., August 30, 1961.
3. Ibid., October 22, 1962 and January 8, 1963.
4. LCUSA *News Bureau*, October 10, 1972.
5. Abner and Martha Batalden, *Because You Cared*, Print-It-Plus, Eagan, Minnesota, 1992, pp. 16-22.
6. Minutes, LWR, January 7, 1964, p. 2, and June 19, 1964, p. 19.
7. NLC *News Bureau*, April 25, 1961.
8. Annual Report, LWR 1966, p. 9.
9. NLC *News Bureau*, March 15, 1966.
10. Ibid., February 4, 1964.
11. LCUSA *News Bureau*, January 7, 1975.
12. Midge Austin Meinertz, ed., *Vietnam Christian Service: Witness in Anguish*, Church World Service, New York, 1975, p. 30.
13. Annual Report, LWR, 1969, p. 23; NLC *News Bureau*, January 27 and September 15, 1966; Minutes, LWR, November 23, 1970.
14. Minutes, LWR, April 11, 1966.
15. LCUSA *News Bureau*, June 17, 1968, and Killen interview by author, January 24, 1993.
16. Confer, Oral History, p. 92, ELCA Archives.
17. Nielsen, Oral History, p. 66, ELCA Archives.
18. Minutes, LWR, June 10, 1968.
19. Annual Report, LWR, 1965, p. 5.

Chapter 7: WITH the People

1. Jerry Aaker, *Partners with the Poor: An Emerging Approach to Relief and Development*, Friendship Press, N.Y. 1993, p. 36.
2. LCUSA *Interchange*, Vol. 10, #5, December, 1977.
3. Bataldens, *Because You Cared*, pp. 27-30.
4. On-site observation by Robert J. Marshall, reported to author in correspondence May 10, 1994.
5. LCUSA *News Bureau*, January 15, 1970, and Minutes, LWR, September 18, 1970, Exhibit U, p. 1.
6. Annual Report, LWR, 1971, and Minutes, January 31, 1978, Ex. L.
7. Annual Reports, LWR, 1970 and 1979.
8. LCUSA *News Bureau*, January 26, 1972.
9. Jonathan Naugle, "Affordable Water for Irrigation: An Experience in Niger," *Waterlines*, July, 1992, reprints available from LWR.

10. "When the Barren Land Blooms" and "Plants to Live," Baramati Agricultural Development Trust pamphlets, and Minutes, LWR, November 12, 1971, and January 24, 1972.

11. Minutes, LWR, January 31, 1978, Exhibit E, and LCUSA *Interchange*, October, 1979, Vol. 12, #4.

12. Asia Case Study: Comprehensive Rural Health Project (India), internal LWR evaluation, 1992.

13. Annual Reports, LWR, 1971 and 1979.

14. Ibid., 1977.

15. Ibid., 1979.

16. LCUSA *Interchange*, July-August, 1975; Minutes, LWR, February 7, 1979, Exhibit T; LCUSA *News Bureau*, September 17, 1972 and September 21, 1973.

17. Annual Reports, LWR, 1972, 1978, 1979.

18. Bataldens, interview by author, August 24, 1993.

19. Aaker, *Partners With the Poor*, pp. 31, 41, 42, and interview by author, August 12, 1993.

20. "Washington Office on Development Policy, A Brief History," staff paper, October, 1991.

21. Confer, Oral History, p. 98, ELCA Archives.

22. Nielsen, Oral History, p. 68, ELCA Archives.

23. Empie, "Inside LWA," Lutheran World Action, 1970, p. 11.

Chapter 8: Support from Church and State

1. Weber, Oral History, pp. 66 and 69, ELCA Archives.

2. Lutz, *Loving Neighbors Far and Near*, Augsburg, 1994, p. 43.

3. Annual Reports, LWR, 1971-1980.

4. Augsburg, Minneapolis, 1994.

5. The *Lutheran*, April, 1994, p. 57.

6. Ibid., October, 1993, NW WA supplement, p. 34c.

7. Wagschal, Edna, correspondence with author, February 19, 1994.

8. Annual Report, LWR, 1973.

9. LCUSA *News Bureau*, November 20, 1972.

10. Minutes, LWR, November 10, 1975, Exhibit K, pp. 3-5.

11. Richard Nixon, message in LWR Minutes, November 23, 1970, Ex. I.

12. Minutes, LWR, September 19, 1973.

13. LCUSA *News Bureau*, March 27, 1973.

14. Ibid., April 17, 1974.

15. "Toward the Development of a U.S. Food Policy," statement by board of LWR, June 18, 1974.

16. LCUSA *News Bureau*, January 23, 1976.

17. "Resolution on National Food Policy," board of LWR, Feb. 8, 1977.

18. LCUSA *News Bureau*, February 11, 1977.

19. Ibid., November 22, 1977.

20. Ibid., December 1, 1977.

21. Ibid., September 28, 1979, and Minutes, LWR, November 21, 1978.

22. Minutes, LWR, July 6, 1978, Exhibit I.

23. Ibid., Exhibit J.

Chapter 9: Fine-Tuning the Management Instrument

1. Confer, Oral History, p. 111, ELCA Archives.

2. Annual Report, LWR, 1988.
3. Nielsen, Oral History, p. 26, ELCA Archives.
4. Confer letter to Nielsen, May 6, 1964, ELCA Archives.
5. Director's Report to Board, December 16, 1983, p. 12.
6. Annual Report, LWR, 1985.
7. Director's Report to Board, March 13, 1989, and LWR Annual Reports for decade.
8. LCUSA *News Bureau*, June 16, 1984.
9. Minutes, LWR, December 11-12, 1979, Exhibit Y.
10. LWR Policy Statement, January 1, 1985, amended Sept. 27, 1991.
11. LCUSA *News Bureau*, June 6, 1984.
12. Ibid., August 1, 1980.
13. Annual Reports, LWR, 1988 and 1989.
14. LCUSA *News Bureau*, February 2, 1982.
15. LWR E LINE through Lutherlink, September 19, 1994.
16. Killen Memo to Sprunger, Attachment to Exhibit C, Director's Report to Board, March 4-5, 1987.
17. Director's Reports to Board, March 1 and May 28-30, 1985.
18. John Soloninka, interview by Ann Fries, March 14, 1994.
19. Eunice Koepke, internal memo, 1993.
20. Report provided author by June Braun, June 13, 1994.
21. Minutes, LWR, September 24, 1993.
22. Director's Report to Board, March 21-22, 1988, Exhibit C, p. 10.
23. Ibid., January 25-26, 1993, Exhibit A, p. 12.
24. Ibid., March 13-14, 1989, Exhibit B, p. 14.
25. Ibid., January 13-14, 1992, Exhibit A, p. 16.
26. Barth, interview by author, January 21, 1994.
27. Compiled from Annual Reports, LWR.
28. Killen, interview by author, May 17, 1994.
29. Killen, memo to author, April 25, 1995.
30. Pedro Veliz, interview by Jeff Whisenant, February 18, 1994.
31. Friendship Press: New York, 1993.
32. Director's Report to Board, March 13-14, 1989, Exhibit B, p. 12.
33. Annual Reports, LWR, 1979-1993.
34. Ibid., 1982 and 1983; Barth interview by author, July 22, 1993.

Chapter 10: Are We Gaining or Losing Ground?

1. The *Lutheran Standard*, January 22, 1980, p. 17.
2. Annual Report, LWR, 1992.
3. Ibid. and Director's Reports, September 14 and December 17, 1984.
4. Marshall in Annual Report, LWR, 1994.
5. Friendship Press: New York, 1991.
6. Director's Report to Board, December 16, 1983, p. 3.
7. LCUSA *News Bureau*, November 19, 1986.
8. Director's Report to Board, May 28-30, 1985, pp. 1, 2.
9. Annual Report, LWR, 1993.
10. Ibid., 1991.
11. *The Lutheran*, November, 1993, p. 49.
12. Director's Report to Board, November 9-10, 1987, Exhibit A, Attachment 2, p. 3.
13. LCUSA *News Bureau*, June 25, 1986.
14. Aguirre, interview by Jeff Whisenant, March 20, 1994.
15. Internal Report of Niger Project Evaluation, 1982.

16. Jonathan Naugle, "On a Technical Note; Hand augured garden wells in Niger," in "Baobab," 1992. Reprints available from LWR.
17. "Project Goes Down the Tubes," undated LWR vignette.
18. Director's Reports to Board, December 16, 1985, Exhibit D, p. 3; March 4-5, 1987, Ex. C, p. 6; January 13-14, 1992, Ex. A, p. 10.
19. "'Micro' Grant Makes 'Macro' Difference," LWR undated vignette.
20. Internal Andean Regional Office Evaluation, LWR, 1982.
21. Ibid., 1987.
22. Internal East Africa Regional Office Report, LWR, 1986.
23. "Asia Case Study: Comprehensive Rural Health Project (India)," in LWR Matching Grant Report for U.S. AID, 1993.
24. Internal Project Evaluations for Asia and Africa, LWR, 1988-1989.
25. LWR Staff Report to Board, January 24-25, 1994, Exhibit A, p. 12.
26. Aaker, *Looking Back...*, HPI, Little Rock, Arkansas, 1994.
27. "Fourth Annual report of the Cooperative Agreement" (LWR-U.S. AID), August 31, 1992.
28. Annual Report, LWR, 1989.
29. Ibid., 1990, and LCUSA *News Bureau*, March 4, 1982.
30. "Togolese Women Who Make Soap," undated LWR vignette.
31. Annual Report, LWR, 1992.
32. "A Project With Bonuses," undated LWR vignette.
33. *The Washington Post*, June 1, 1993.

Chapter 11: LWR in the New World Disorder

1. Issue Paper, "LWR Work in the Area of Conflict Resolution," June 14-15, 1991, and Director's Report to Board, January 13-14, 1992, Exhibit A, p. 13.
2. Annual Report, LWR, 1991, and report from R. Wesley Newswanger, May 20, 1993.
3. Various staff reports from Centre in LWR files.
4. Mark Duffield and John Prendergast, *Neutrality and Humanitarian Assistance, the Emergency Relief Desk and Cross-Border Operation into Eritrea and Tigray*, Center of Concern, Wash. D.C., 1993.
5. Director's Report to Board, January 14, 1991, Exhibit A, pp. 1, 2.
6. Ibid., September 27-28, 1990.
7. LCUSA *News Bureau*, October 23, 1986.
8. Director's Report to Board, January 13-14, 1992, Exhibit A, p. 1.
9. *Humanitarianism Under Siege: A Critical Review of Operation Lifeline Sudan*, The Red Sea Press, Washington, D.C., 1991.
10. Minutes, LWR, September 27, 1991, p. 4.
11. Minear, *Humanitarianism Under Siege....*, p. 150.
12. Larry Minear and Thomas G. Weiss, *Humanitarian Action in Times of War*, Lynne Rienner, Boulder and London, 1993.
13. "LWR Work in the Area of Conflict Resolution," June 14-15, 1991.
14. Wolford, letter to contributors, July 16, 1994.
15. Emmanuel Ohajah, Twin Cities' *Star Tribune*, April 15, 1994, 16 A.
16. LCUSA *News Bureau*, February 10, 1986, and Confer, Oral History, p. 8, ELCA Archives.
17. Director's Report to Board, September 25, 1992, Exhibit A, p. 25.
18. Annual Report, LWR, 1988.
19. Director's Report to Board, September 25, 1992, Exhibit A, p. 24.
20. LCUSA *Interchange*, October, 1979.

21. "A Fresh Start: New Paths for U.S. Economic Policy Toward Central America," Central America Working Group, Washington, D.C., 1993.
22. LCUSA *News Bureau*, June 12, 1981.
23. Director's Report to Board, May 31-June 2, 1983, p. 1.
24. Annual Report, LWR, 1985.
25. LCUSA *News Bureau*, March 16, 1983.
26. Ibid., February 10, 1986.
27. 2 Cor. 14, 15 and Aaker, *Partners With the Poor*, p. 78.
28. Lutz, *Loving Neighbors Far and Near*, p. 70.
29. Annual Report, LWR, 1990.
30. "LWR Strategy FY 1994," in staff report to Board, September 24, 1993, Exhibit A, p. 1, and Director's Report to Board, January 24-25, 1994, Exhibit A, p. 4.
31. Annual Report, LWR, 1988.
32. Ibid., 1989.
33. "Living Earth" and "Don Santos and His Wonderful Neem Trees," LWR undated vignettes.
34. Annual Report, LWR, 1989.
35. Sell, interview by author, August 18, 1994.
36. Wolford, "The Relationship Between the Christian Faith and Relief, Development, and Advocacy Work," statement to Board, 1993.
37. "LWR, the Fabric of the Future," study document, May 18, 1994.
38. Wolford, "The Relationship....," statement to Board, 1993.
39. Weber, Oral History, p. 72, ELCA Archives.
40. Moll, letter to Confer, October 10, 1949, ELCA Archives.
41. Robert Cottingham, interview by author, August 26, 1993, and Bataldens, *Because You Cared*, p. 100.
42. Busche, Oral History, p. 161, ELCA Archives.
43. Jeff Whisenant, interview by author, September 20, 1994, and Bataldens, *Because You Cared*, p. 101.
44. Carl Mau, letter to author, October 10, 1994.
45. Bataldens, *Because You Cared*, p. 101.

Index